The Pocke

Uni

Principles of UX

100 Timeless Strategies to Create Positive Interactions between People and Technology

Irene Pereyra

Define

Research

Design

Validate

Most jobs have an easy-to-understand title you can quickly mention and move on from with no risk of confusion, and most job titles don't require lengthy explanations. I'm a photographer. I'm a teacher. I'm a zoologist. People nod, say something polite like "That must be interesting!" take a sip of their drink and continue the conversation. "I am a UX designer," however, almost always results in raised eyebrows followed by a rambling monologue where I try to explain the complexity, expansiveness, and evolving nature of the field.

"You know what an architect does? UX designers—or user experience designers—are basically architects, but instead of designing physical structures, we design digital structures. And just as architects don't actually physically build the buildings they design, we also rely on programmers and developers to build the digital structures we design."

However incomplete my architect analogy may be, user experience design is not a new concept. Some claim the term was first coined by Don Norman in 1993 for his new job as User Experience Architect at Apple, whereas others say it was first described in a 1987 usability engineering journal by John Whiteside and Dennis Wixon.

The exact origin of the term may be debatable, but the fact that the practice of user experience design goes back a long time is not.

When the Greek physician Hippocrates wrote how a surgeon's tools should be arranged for optimal use in operations; or mechanical engineer Frederick Winslow Taylor analyzed workflows in order to increase productivity while reducing work related injuries; or media mogul Walt Disney and his team of "Imagineers" put themselves in their guest's shoes so they could create magical and immersive park experiences, they were all acting as user experience designers.

Perhaps the best predigital-era example of someone thinking of the user experience comes from 1955. Industrial designer Henry Dreyfuss famously wrote, "When the point of contact between the product and the people becomes a point of friction, then the designer has failed. On the other hand, if people are made safer, more comfortable, more eager to purchase, more efficient—or just plain happier—by contact with the product, then the designer has succeeded."

Now if you imagine that the product he mentioned could also be a digital product, like email or an online dating app, or a transaction, like buying airline tickets or shopping for a new pair of shoes, and you replace the word *people* with *users*, you basically have the framework for user experience design today.

But here's the catch. Ask ten different people to define user experience design today, and you'll receive ten different answers. Unlike architecture, which has had thousands of years to mature and to be defined, we are still in the infancy of defining what this field actually is. Not to mention that experiences are inherently subjective, and that we design digital services, products, and tools—not experiences—that we hope will result in the intended experience.

To make matters worse, during my many years of teaching user experience design, I realized a lot of the books and articles that cover this topic tend to be written from the outside-in, with the author compiling a list of examples that describe a process they were not actually a part of—a theoretical utopia. It's also almost always written in a way that makes it seem like there is a perfect way of doing things, and if you don't do it that way you're doing it wrong. But the perfect UX process does not exist.

There is no one definition of UX design. The same job title can mean different things at different companies, and the answer to almost every question is "it depends."

This book is not a chronological retelling of the history of user experience design. It is also not a technical how-to book that will show you how to become a perfect user experience designer one step at a time. It's a philosophical anthology of case studies, situations, problems, and contradictions I've encountered across more than fifteen years of working on real-world client projects that will teach you how to think, rather than tell you what to do. And in the spirit of the internet, it's up to you whether you want to go through these sequentially or jump around to topics you find interesting.

But there is one thing we can all agree on: User experience is about users. So let's start there. Who are they anyway? And why should we care? Understanding the needs, goals, desires, and motivations of these real human beings—everyone who interacts with and is affected by these digital products—is the first step in getting closer to untangling the contradictory field that is user experience design.

01. The user comes first.

We kick off every project with these pivotal questions: Who is it for (the audience)? Why will they use it (the goal)? And how will they use it (the context of use)?

- Keeping human beings—or "users"—at the core of design allows us to steer clear from misguided decisions, potentially coming from either stakeholders' personal biases or, even worse, designers' assumptions.
- Luckily, putting the user first doesn't require complex procedures. It simply means listening more, talking less, asking smart questions, being curious, and showing empathy.
- During the early stages of my career, I worked on the web interface for an Electronic Arts' college football game. But I didn't know anything about American football. So, to ensure I was on the right track, I talked with some college friends who were huge football enthusiasts. This user-focused approach made the final product so much better, proving that it beats relying solely on personal assumptions.
- In essence, involving users from the start of the design process greatly improves the final user experience (see Principle 57).

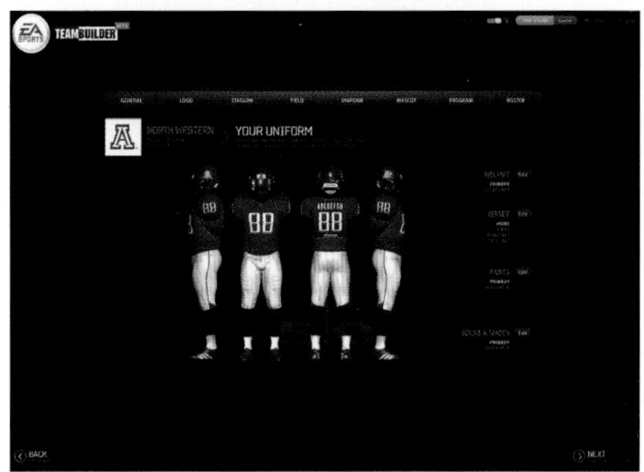

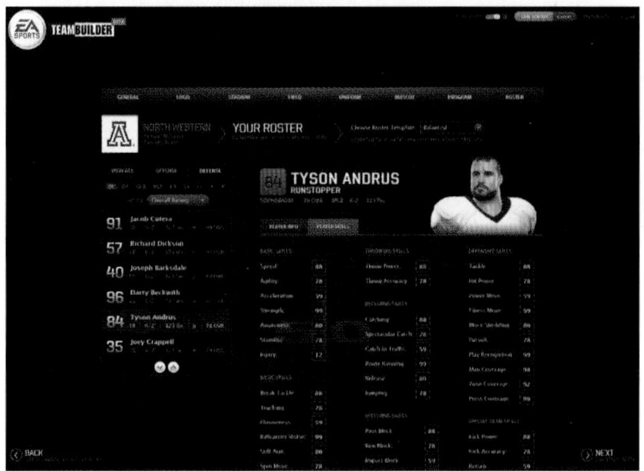

NCAA Football 11, released in 2010, featured user-customizable Teambuilder options online.

02. Work on UX and UI simultaneously.

Exploring the "UX versus UI" conversation allows us to understand their subtle differences and the crucial roles they hold, particularly considering the industry's evolution since the early 2000s.

- In the past, all online design was simply termed "web design." As technology evolved, roles became more defined to cover a variety of devices and contexts.
- UX design is like the foundation or blueprint of a building, focusing on user needs, behaviors, and contexts.
- UI design enhances this foundation, choosing aesthetics and functionality, akin to selecting a building's interior decor and accessibility features.
- To achieve a balanced, effective, and appealing final product, it's essential to integrate UX and UI from the start, letting each play to its strength.
- In essence, collaborating between UX and UI from the start creates a cohesive and effective product vision, allowing for a full integration of both functionality and aesthetics.

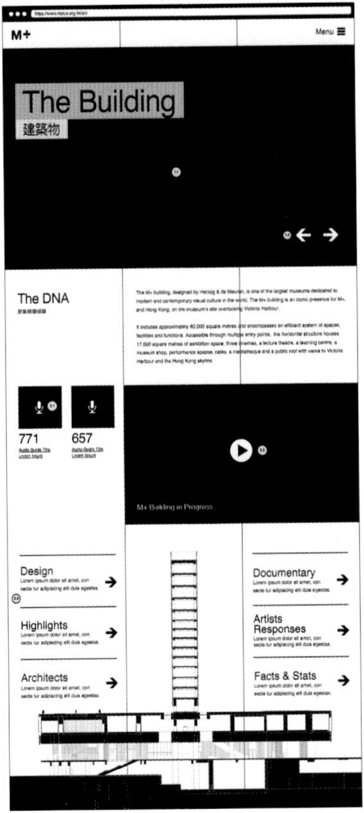

M+

Menu

The Building

建築物

The DNA

The M+ building, designed by Herzog & de Meuron, is one of the largest museums dedicated to modern and contemporary visual culture in the world. The M+ building is an iconic presence for M+, and Hong Kong, on the museum's site overlooking Victoria Harbour.

It includes approximately 60,000 square metres and encompasses an efficient system of spaces, facilities and functions. Accessible through multiple entry points, the horizontal structure houses 17,000 square metres of exhibition space, three cinemas, a lecture theatre, a learning centre, a museum shop, performance spaces, cafes, a mediatheque and a public roof with views to Victoria Harbour and the Hong Kong skyline.

771

657

M+ Building in Progress

Design
Lorem ipsum dolor sit amet, con secte tur adipiscing elit duis egestas.

Highlights
Lorem ipsum dolor sit amet, con secte tur adipiscing elit duis egestas.

Architects
Lorem ipsum dolor sit amet, con secte tur adipiscing elit duis egestas.

Documentary
Lorem ipsum dolor sit amet, con secte tur adipiscing elit duis egestas.

Artists Responses
Lorem ipsum dolor sit amet, con secte tur adipiscing elit duis egestas.

Facts & Stats
Lorem ipsum dolor sit amet, con secte tur adipiscing elit duis egestas.

The "Building" page of M+ museum details its design by Herzog & de Meuron, progressing from UX wireframes to final UI.

03. UI makes or breaks usability.

Usability is often linked to UX, but UI elements like layout and typography can greatly affect it, as highlighted by the 2000 U.S. presidential election.

- Usability is paramount in design, determining if a user can effectively achieve their goal with a product.
- While UX focuses on the overall user experience, it's the UI's responsibility to dictate direct user interactions through layout, typography, and other elements.
- The 2000 U.S. presidential election highlighted significant usability issues in both UX (e.g., confusing instructions, inconsistent voting mechanics) and UI (e.g., biased order of candidates, poor typography).
- Usability encompasses more than just user experience or ease of use; it must be considered by both UX and UI designers throughout the design process (see Principle 75).
- Proper usability testing could have prevented the infamous "butterfly" ballot debacle, possibly changing the outcome of the election.

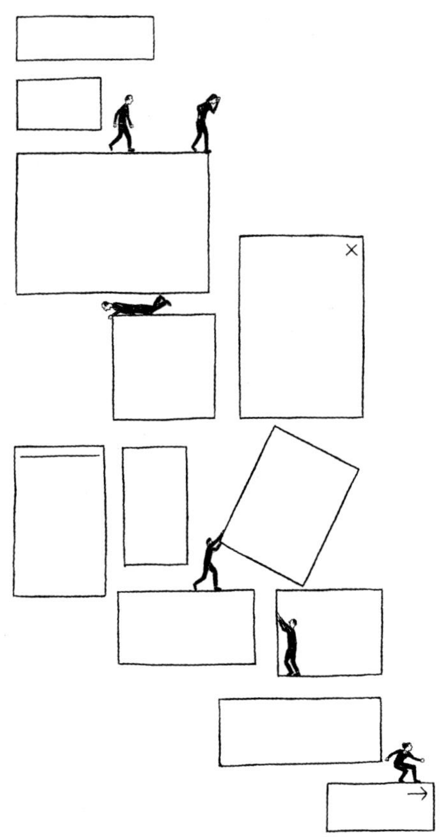

04. Always surpass expectations.

An amazing user experience goes beyond functionality; it surprises and delights, much like the unexpected pleasures of Singapore's Changi Airport versus the dreariness of New York City's LaGuardia Airport. While both airports serve the same basic purpose, one is substantially better than the other.

- Simply focusing on usability and functionality in design isn't enough; it must also be memorable and distinctive.
- While a product must fundamentally work, in today's saturated market, mere functionality isn't enough; it must stand out.
- Memorable experiences combine wow-factor elements with immersive interactions that engage users seamlessly.
- But most importantly, achieving a state of flow, or complete immersion, combined with innovative features, is key to exceeding user expectations.
- In essence, surpassing expectations means going beyond basic functionality to create memorable and delightful experiences. This involves integrating unique features, immersive interactions, and innovation to engage users seamlessly and leave a lasting impression (see Principle 41).

our story

placing & growing talent around the world

True Search
We place executives and other strategic talent for the world's most innovative organizations.

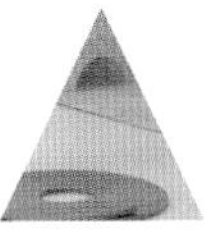

Thrive
We've built powerful talent management technology for enterprises, investment firms, and recruiters.

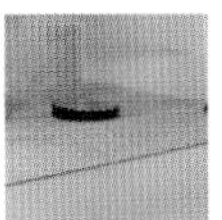

Synthesis
Helping leaders and teams reach their full potential, make better talent decisions, and increase value creation.

We designed an interactive model for True, where each letter reacts to cursor movement, and scrolling reveals dynamic background imagery.

05. Design is not neutral.

In UX design, without a clear-cut ethics code, it's crucial for designers to trust their own moral judgment, especially when navigating both clear and subtle ethical challenges.

- Early internet scams were overt, but today's web uses subtle tactics by legitimate companies to manipulate users for gain.
- While many professions have ethical guidelines, the design field lacks a universal ethics code.

- "Dark patterns" or "deceptive patterns," for example, are intentionally crafted to mislead users, ranging from benign to harmful tactics.
- But without a clear framework, designers often find themselves in moral dilemmas, deciding on their own what's right or wrong.
- In short, ethical considerations are paramount. Recognizing these challenges, promoting ethical principles, and making informed decisions to avoid harm or misinformation are essential responsibilities for designers in the absence of universal ethical guidelines.

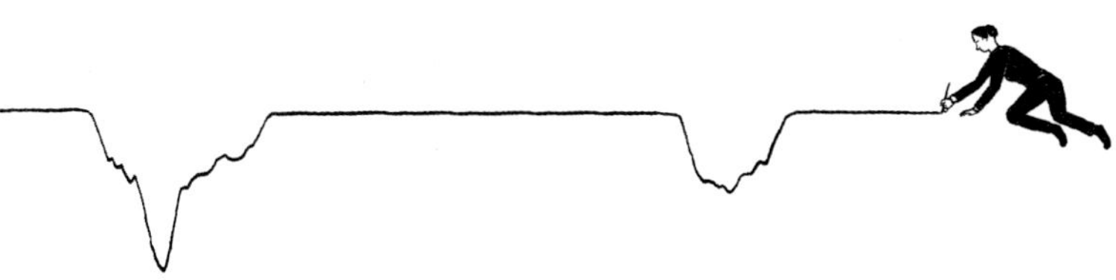

06. Words matter.

Effective UX design hinges significantly on skillful writing. Good UX copy is written to be felt and is the opposite of technical jargon. It's meant to evoke emotion, while simultaneously removing all ambiguity.

- Users want task-focused, conversational interactions online, so we should aim for web copy that's easy to digest: with simple language, clear labels, and concise content (see Principle 75).
- People also love lists—like this one that you're reading right now—so use them!
- Bonus points if you address the user directly with "you"; it centers the narrative around them and their needs.
- Once done, be sure to edit ruthlessly and test your copy by reading it aloud. If it doesn't sound natural or conversational, it needs more refining.
- In essence, crafting thoughtful UX copy is about bridging clarity with emotion, ensuring that users not only understand but also connect with the narrative presented.

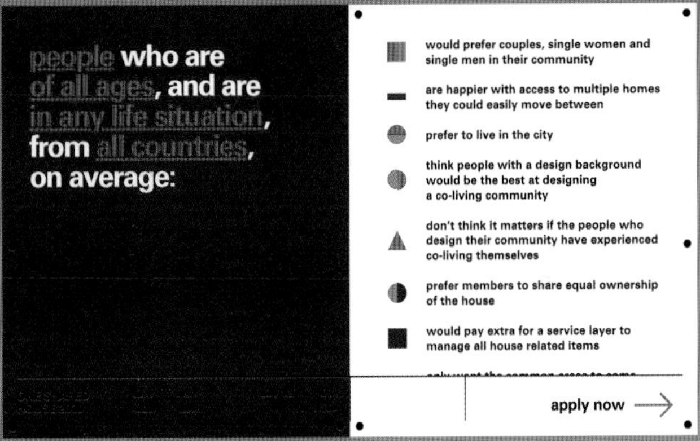

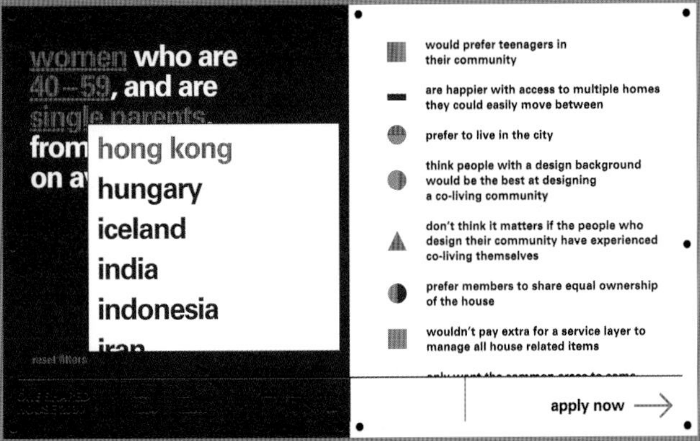

people who are of all ages, and are in any life situation, from all countries, on average:

would prefer couples, single women and single men in their community

are happier with access to multiple homes they could easily move between

prefer to live in the city

think people with a design background would be the best at designing a co-living community

don't think it matters if the people who design their community have experienced co-living themselves

prefer members to share equal ownership of the house

would pay extra for a service layer to manage all house related items

apply now →

women who are 40–59, and are single parents, from

on a

hong kong

hungary

iceland

india

indonesia

iran

reset filters

would prefer teenagers in their community

are happier with access to multiple homes they could easily move between

prefer to live in the city

think people with a design background would be the best at designing a co-living community

don't think it matters if the people who design their community have experienced co-living themselves

prefer members to share equal ownership of the house

wouldn't pay extra for a service layer to manage all house related items

apply now →

We designed an interface for SPACE10/IKEA's "One Shared House 2030" survey, enabling swift data filtering via conversational language.

07. Visual metaphors communicate the fastest.

Images are processed by our brains 60,000 times quicker than text. They're interpreted through our "mental models," which are simplified understandings of the world. Visual metaphors use these models to allow audiences to connect using familiar symbols (see Principle 62).

- Visual metaphors have a universal appeal that cuts through cultural and linguistic barriers. They evoke emotions and create connections that words alone might struggle to achieve.
- In our "Messages for Japan" project for Google, we strategically chose the cherry blossom tree, which represents hope and renewal, resonating deeply with the emotions of the time following the 2011 earthquake and tsunami in Japan.
- The response was heartwarming. The cherry blossom tree, adorned with messages from around the world, amassed over 50,000 notes, turning a symbol into a beacon of global unity.
- Beyond emotional engagement, this project raised five million dollars in donations. It underscored the effectiveness of visual metaphors in not just drawing attention, but also spurring action and creating meaningful change.

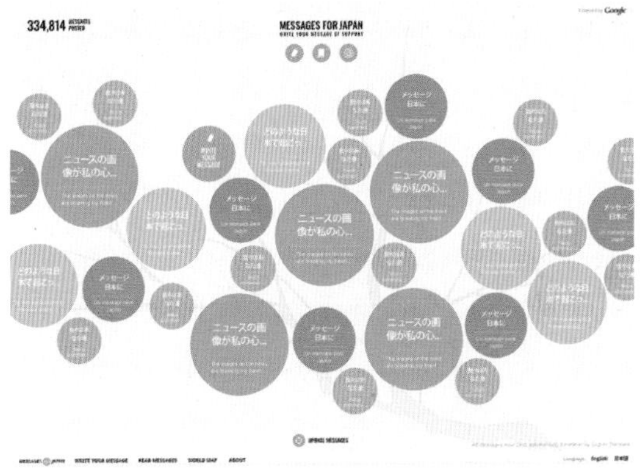

Google Japan's interactive experience enabled global users to leave multilingual messages on a blossoming digital cherry tree post-tsunami in 2011.

08. Attractive products are more usable.

Exploring the balance between usability and aesthetics in interface design reveals an interesting insight: users often link beauty with functionality. Essentially, if it looks good, we're more likely to think it works well.

- In a 1995 study by Kurosu and Kashimura where they tested various different ATM interfaces, they discovered participants equated beauty with functionality, often favoring looks over actual ease of use.
- Their findings revealed a strong aesthetic-usability effect: people generally feel that visually appealing products are more user-friendly, even if that's not always the case.
- Interestingly, if a beautiful product has minor usability hitches, users tend to be more forgiving.
- That said, while a great design can earn some leeway, a completely non-functional product will always hit a user's limit, regardless of its aesthetics (see Principle 13).
- If there is a real lesson to be learned here, it's not that we should focus on only making things beautiful while ignoring usability, it's to understand why we should focus on both.

A close-up of our self-produced NU:RO analog watch that tells the time in the middle of the hourglass. It's not the most intuitive design, but it's certainly a beautiful one.

09. People remember the unusual.

Balancing familiar elements with fresh innovations is essential in design. Standing out while ensuring comfort can greatly enhance user engagement and memorability. Ultimately, mixing what's known with a hint of uniqueness can transform user experiences.

- The MAYA principle (an acronym for Most Advanced Yet Acceptable), developed by French American industrial designer Raymond Loewy, emphasizes the importance of merging the familiar with the new, aiming to captivate users while also comforting them with elements they recognize.
- The Von Restorff effect, stemming from 1933 studies by German psychologist Hedwig von Restorff, suggests that standout items—marked by distinct features—are notably more memorable, highlighting the power of uniqueness.
- Both principles highlight a key insight for designers: striking a balance between familiarity and novelty can significantly enhance user engagement and product memorability.
- In other words, to be memorable, sometimes the best strategy is simply doing the opposite of the norm (see Principle 15).

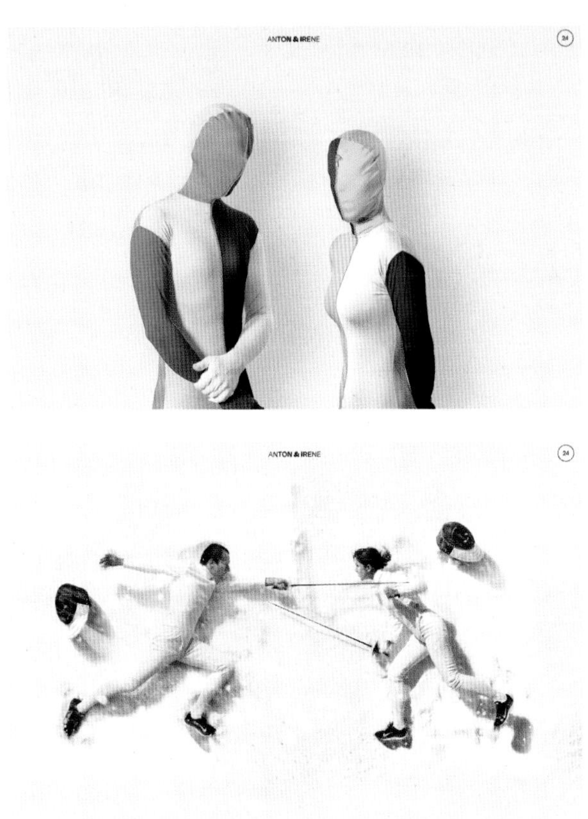

Our studio's unique, interactive homepage and bio images stand out distinctly in the agency landscape, enhancing memorability.

10. First and last items are remembered most.

In 1885, German psychologist Hermann Ebbinghaus identified the "serial position effect," showing we mainly remember items at the start and end of a sequence. The first items enter our long-term memory, while the last ones stay in short-term memory, causing middle items to be forgotten.

- In UX design, where you place information can make a huge difference in how users interact with and remember content.
- Therefore, it's crucial to position essential data or calls to action at the beginning or end of a sequence for the best user recall and engagement.
- But it's not just about showing info, it's about arranging it so users remember the vital bits and let the less important stuff fade.
- By using memory-based strategies, we can shape user interaction and direct their attention to what truly counts.
- In UX design, knowing the serial position effect helps you place information where it's most likely to be recalled.

The "Time During Covid-19" project elicits feedback about pandemic experiences at the end of a virtual tunnel.

11. Less is more.

The design mantra "less is more" remains a hot debate in the design world. Before discussing it, many people believe in it. Yet after exploring both sides, most change their minds. Ultimately, there's no definitive answer; sometimes less is more, and sometimes it's not.

- "Less is more" is a debated design cliché, with its roots in midcentury architecture. The phrase emerged as a response against ornate designs, advocating for minimalism and functionality.
- In UX design, keeping things simple is often preferred because too much information can cause mistakes, especially during complicated tasks.
- So for tasks like ticket purchasing, or anything else that requires multiple inputs and steps, a minimalist design reduces cognitive load and improves usability.
- While ornate designs have their place in UX (see Principle 12), for complex interactions and long processes, simplicity is key, and "less is more."

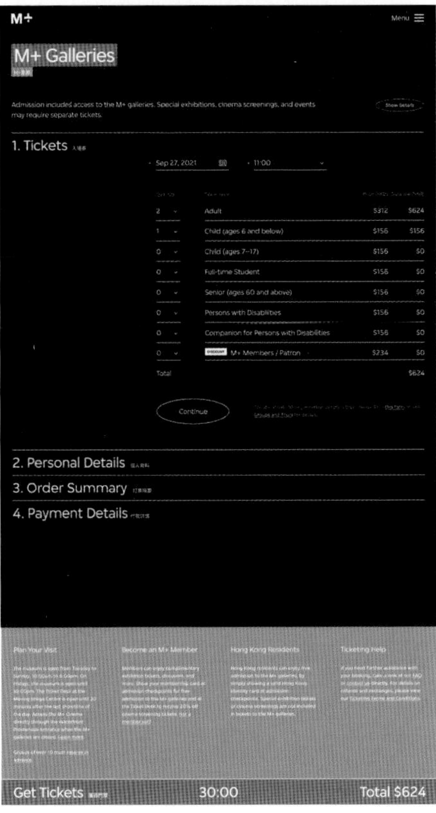

We streamlined the M+ museum's ticket purchasing process, ensuring simplicity and minimizing error potential.

12. Less is a bore.

Two decades after Mies van der Rohe's "less is more" mantra (see Principle 11), architect Robert Venturi countered with "less is a bore." This challenged the reigning minimalist modernist architecture, applauding the ornate designs of earlier classical eras, promoting flair and maximalism.

- Early web designs had unique personalities that faded in the 2000s, leading to a widespread uniformity in UX design.
- The ubiquitous sameness in design allows those who dare to be different to stand out using maximalism.
- Maximalist design can evoke strong emotions through bold choices in colors, patterns, fonts, and interactions.
- Successful maximalism ensures design functionality; it isn't about clutter but rather adding meaningful, engaging elements.
- In essence, where minimalism is subtle, maximalism celebrates diversity, giving users a refreshing experience amidst digital uniformity.

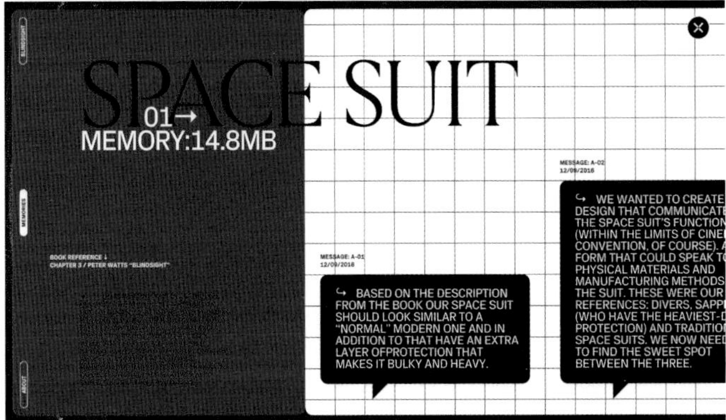

SPACE SUIT
01→
MEMORY:14.8MB
BOOK REFERENCE ↓
CHAPTER 3 / PETER WATTS "BLINDSIGHT"
MESSAGE: A-01
12/09/2016
BASED ON THE DESCRIPTION FROM THE BOOK OUR SPACE SUIT SHOULD LOOK SIMILAR TO A "NORMAL" MODERN ONE AND IN ADDITION TO THAT HAVE AN EXTRA LAYER OFPROTECTION THAT MAKES IT BULKY AND HEAVY.
MESSAGE: A-02
12/09/2016

Blindsight's interactive experience employs a maximalist approach, utilizing vivid art and spiral interactions inspired by the protagonist's memory voyage.

13. Provide feedback quickly or else.

In the television series *Halt and Catch Fire*, set during the 1980s PC era, a 400-millisecond response was touted as crucial for user engagement. Yet this figure, referenced from a 1982 IBM study, was about enhancing programmer productivity, not user engagement.

- Speed can often outweigh aesthetics, making a swift yet basic design memorable for users. In most cases, ugly but fast is better than pretty but slow.
- Jakob Nielsen emphasizes three key response-time limits: 0.1 second for immediate system feedback, 1 second to preserve user's focus, and 10 seconds to retain engagement. Besides that, users should be notified at 2 seconds of processing, and by 5 seconds, the expected wait duration should be indicated.
- Yet, occasionally, introducing a deliberate pause in user interactions can be crucial (see Principle 14). Recognizing when to prioritize speed or introduce intentional delays can define the user experience.
- Striking a balance between speed and purposeful interaction can be the key to an engaging and memorable user experience.

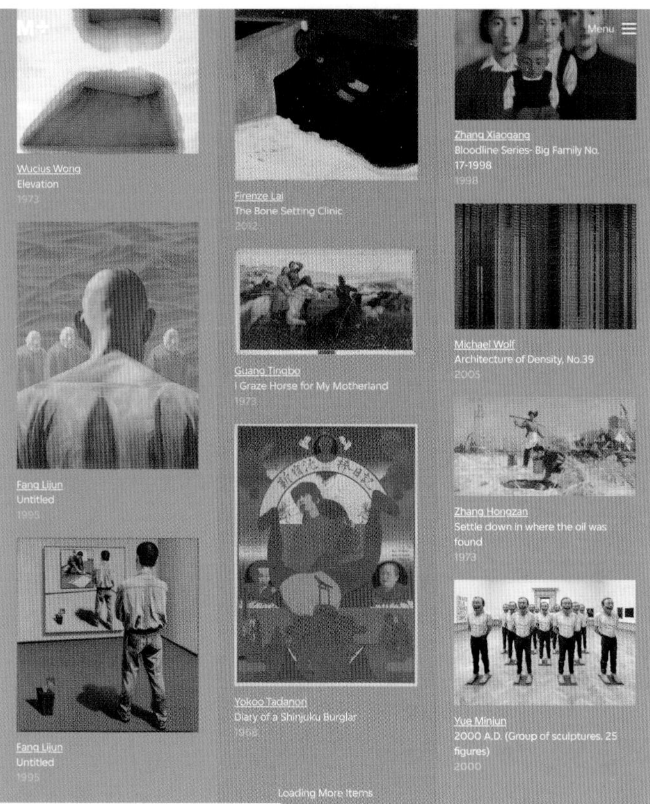

M+ museum's online collection uses endless scroll, signaling users when rapid scrolling or slow connections delay content loading.

14. Friction isn't always bad.

Balancing friction with user experience reveals that strategic obstacles can deter rushed decisions and unexpected outcomes. While designers usually prioritize seamless interactions, intentional hurdles matter when choices have notable consequences.

- While UX designers work hard to provide smooth user journeys, there are moments when a "speed bump" is intentionally added, especially for actions that can have lasting consequences.
- These carefully placed "speed bumps" serve as crucial reminders, ensuring users pause and consider their actions rather than breezing through on autopilot.
- However, many of us have grown so used to pop-ups, for example, that we barely notice them, as highlighted by a Böhme and Köpsell study.
- So, when crafting digital experiences it's essential to strike a balance: streamline where possible (see Principle 13), but also introduce friction when it aids in user protection and promotes thoughtful decision-making.

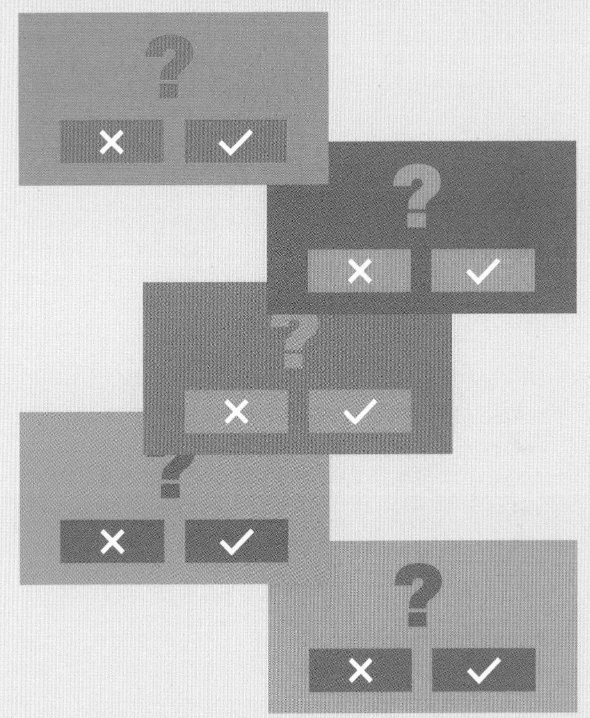

15. First impressions matter.

A first impression forms in just ten seconds. Microsoft's research found that users will exit a web page if its value isn't clear within that time frame. That's because users know that they will easily be able to find whatever it is that they need somewhere else.

- Design surprisingly trumps content in the initial user impression, making it an integral force in anchoring user trust and invigorating further exploration. Any misstep in layout, typography, or color schemes can deter users regardless of content quality (see Principle 8).
- Great design isn't just nice to look at. It builds trust and keeps people around. Every bit of those first 10 seconds has to really spark and grab attention.
- Therefore, it's important to understand where the majority of user navigation commences from and invest design energy there.
- In other words, great design not only gets people to trust you, but it's also what makes them want to stick around. And since we know we only get ten seconds to make a first impression, they should count.

The homepage concept became central in redesigning Shantell Martin's website, prioritizing a user's key entry point with significant design focus.

16. UX design isn't timeless.

Exploring Dieter Rams's design principles, it's clear that what works for industrial design might need a rethink when it comes to the ever-changing world of UX.

- Rams had a solid list with his "10 Principles of Good Design." But when we hit UX territory, one principle doesn't ring true: the idea of "long-lasting" design.
- That's because hardware changes at lightning speed. Remember when touchscreens felt futuristic? Or the first time you interacted with augmented reality or virtual reality? These changes directly affect the user experience, and how the subsequent interfaces get designed.
- Software's no different. Imagine showing someone from 20 years ago a hamburger menu icon. They wouldn't know how to interact with it (see Principle 82).
- But there's a silver lining: we humans adapt fast. Every tech leap means we learn and get ready for the next big thing. So, while that means UX might not be timeless, it's always evolving, just like us.

17. Nothing lasts forever.

In fifteen years of working in this space, we've seen our designs endure or change drastically. The main influence isn't design evolution or tech progress, but client leadership and their turnover.

- Longevity in design often mirrors the stability of client-side leadership; our designs maintain their originality under the vigilant eyes of consistent leadership who initially commissioned it.
- Digital natives like Google and Spotify tend to value consistent design. They make changes sparingly to avoid user alienation.
- On the other hand, nondigital native entities often update their designs with each leadership change—ambitious executives who are eager to leave their mark—often without a comprehensive understanding of user needs.
- Design lifespan often depends on the tenure of its decision-makers. So, sometimes we have to let go of designs we once loved. I've come to terms with it. Instead of seeing past projects as my "babies," I now view them as my "ex-husbands."

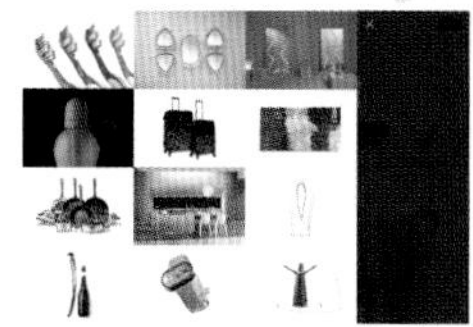

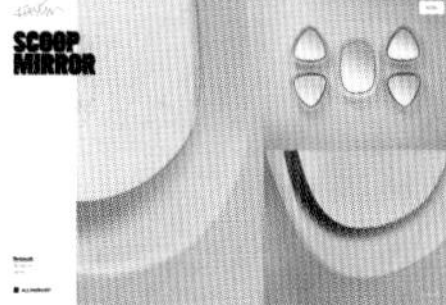

The Karim Rashid website, commissioned by Rashid himself, has thrived and remained unchanged for over ten years, reflecting his steady leadership.

18. Accessibility first.

A website with closed captions aids both people who are deaf and users in noisy places, and enhanced contrast benefits people who are visually impaired as well as people using the interface in bright lighting conditions. Accessibility is essential for some, and it's useful for all of us.

- Despite its widespread benefits, a staggering 98 percent of websites fail to meet accessibility standards, according to a 2020 report by WebAIM.

- There's some good news though. The Americans with Disabilities Act and the upcoming European Accessibility Act are putting down some ground rules, and gently nudging designers and developers toward creating more inclusive digital spaces.
- But making products accessible isn't just a designer's job. From ensuring website text is legible for screen readers to selecting accessible libraries, developers have an important role to play too.
- It's on us, however, the UX designers, to champion accessibility in our designs (see Principle 65). By creating with everyone in mind, we improve the user experience for all.

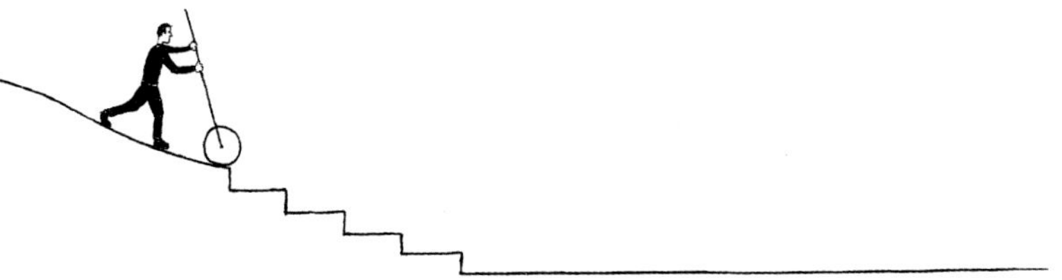

19. Allow for differences in digital literacy.

In today's digital world, literacy goes beyond just reading and writing. It includes the ability to use, assess, and produce various digital content and tools, which are crucial for tasks like scheduling vaccinations or handling taxes.

- Marc Prensky's terms "digital native" and "digital immigrant" highlight the divide between those born into the digital age and those who adapted to it later in life.
- Designing for digital immigrants means focusing on the basics: intuitive interactions, straightforward language, and pacing that puts them in control.
- Tools like color coding can act as memory aids, and offering diverse learning routes ensures everyone finds their footing.
- By prioritizing this inclusive approach, we're not just designing for ease of use, but building confidence for those feeling a step behind in our digital world.
- An inclusive design bridges the gap between digital natives and immigrants, ensuring that everyone, regardless of their tech savviness, feels empowered and confident in the digital space.

20. Take extra care of seniors.

When it comes to designing digital products, catering to the needs of seniors, often considered digital immigrants (see Principle 19), is essential. These users, introduced to technology later in life, may face insecurities when navigating new digital interfaces.

- Seniors, being digital immigrants, often feel insecure with new digital products.
- Seniors generally need more time to process interface information, value clear instructions, and take actions cautiously.
- Design choices that greatly help seniors include minimizing icons (see Principle 82), emphasizing clear labels, and avoiding mandatory account creation.
- While these tweaks are senior-centric, they make digital spaces friendlier for everyone, championing inclusivity for all users. Designing with seniors in mind ensures usability for all digital immigrants, not just the elderly.

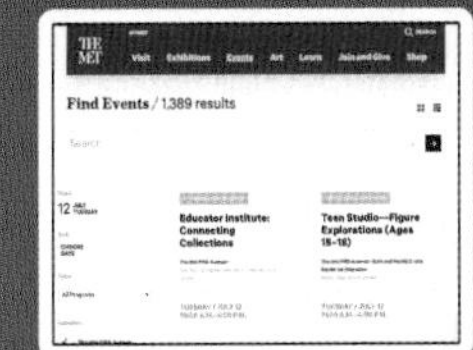

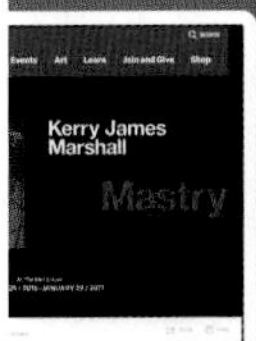

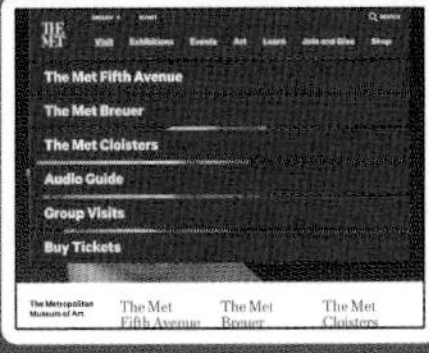

Met Museum's website prioritizes ease of use, especially for seniors, with bold, user-friendly design across desktop, mobile, and tablet screens.

21. Children are not small adults.

When designing interfaces for children, it's vital to understand their unique behaviors and needs rather than just simplifying, colorizing, or "dumbing down" the interface.

- Kids navigate content differently than adults; they're all about exploring, not just following a straight path.
- Therefore when designing for children, it's essential to strike a sweet spot between guiding young users and giving them freedom to explore and play.
- However, recognizing their developmental stages is key; for instance, six- to eleven-year-olds are diving deep into logic, so looking at games that spark their thinking can provide valuable insights for creating suitable interfaces for this age group.
- A good interface for kids understands their mindset, and unique developmental stage, while delivering an engaging mix of challenge and fun.
- In essence, tailoring digital experiences to children means diving into their world and balancing playful exploration with age-appropriate guidance and content.

22. Design for learnability.

"Learnability" in UX design is about making it easy for users to get the hang of new interactions. It's more than just usability; it's creating an experience where users pick things up as they go, learning while they interact with what's in front of them.

- High learnability enables users to grasp novel interactions without any training or instructions (see Principle 19), which means that the user should subconsciously absorb how to navigate and utilize the interface, while interacting with it.
- If you come up with something that users have likely not encountered before, don't be alarmed if the initial usability isn't high right off the bat. Worry instead about designing a system that allows users to ambiently learn it while interacting with it.
- When in doubt, we can take inspiration from game designers, who masterfully mingle complexity and feedback into an immersive journey where you're learning without even realizing it.
- Aim for creating an interface that allows users to naturally learn and improve, even if initial usability isn't perfect.

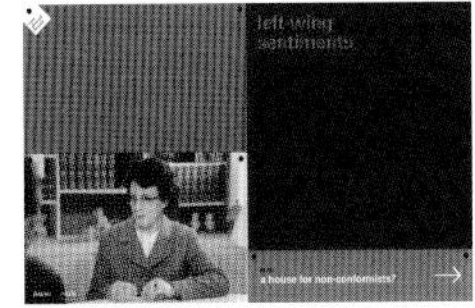

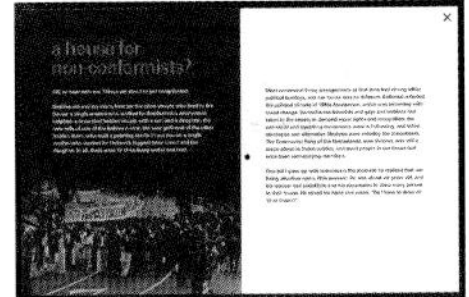

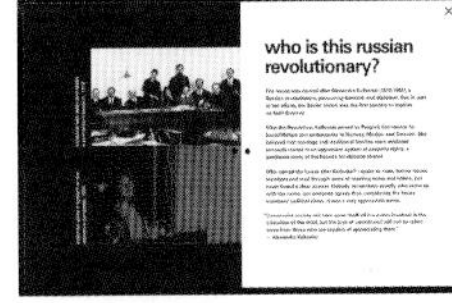

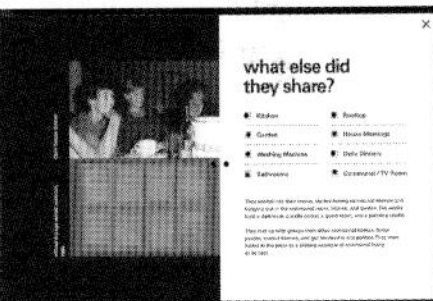

"One Shared House" enhances UX learnability by blending interactive, optional content with a traditional documentary viewing experience.

23. Don't just design for novices.

Designing a digital platform that aids both new users and expert "power users" requires a balance between simplicity for beginners and depth for experienced users.

- Often, when designing, we tend to focus on first-time visitors (see Principle 15). But what happens when users return frequently? Or are experts at using the product already?
- For those dipping their toes in for the first time, a neat and intuitive interface is their best friend.
- On the flip side, our seasoned users are hunting for advanced features and a bit more control to flex their expertise or speed up their process.
- The trick is merging the beginner-friendly with the pro-level stuff, ensuring neither feels out of place and everyone's cruising smoothly.
- However, it's important to note that power features should always be optional—tucked away but easily accessible for those looking for more speed or control.

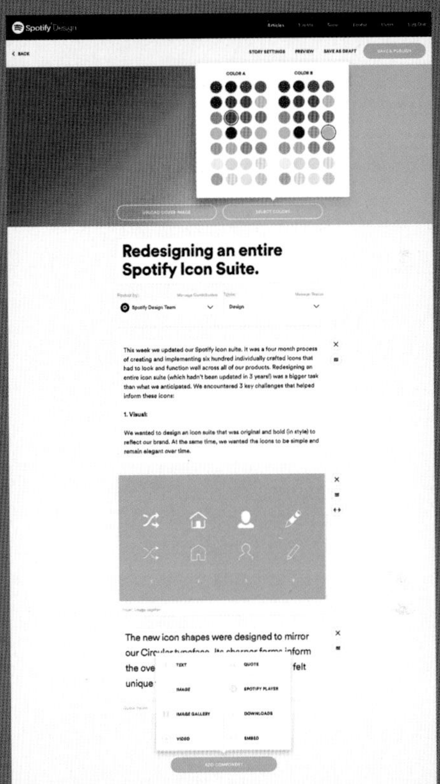

The CMS we designed for Spotify allowed a select group of people within Spotify to publish content on the Spotify website without having to involve any designers or developers.

24. Make the choice easy.

Hick's Law examines the impact of choice on decision-making and highlights the importance in UX design of striking a balance between offering options and ensuring easy decision-making.

- Hick's Law applies to situations in which decisions are not that important (like choosing the right cheese), but it doesn't apply to decisions that carry heavier consequences (like choosing between universities or job offers).
- As UX designers, our job isn't to cut choices but to curate them, making sure users aren't swamped with too many minor decisions.
- It's all about balancing the lineup of options so users have a sense of control without feeling overwhelmed.
- When designing interfaces, it's crucial to have a system that simplifies tasks and eliminates unnecessary options for the user.
- Choices should have clear intent, and users should be shielded from getting overwhelmed by minor details.

Who are you designing for?
choose persona

Who are you designing for?
Nick

Who is Nick with?
choose persona and make selection

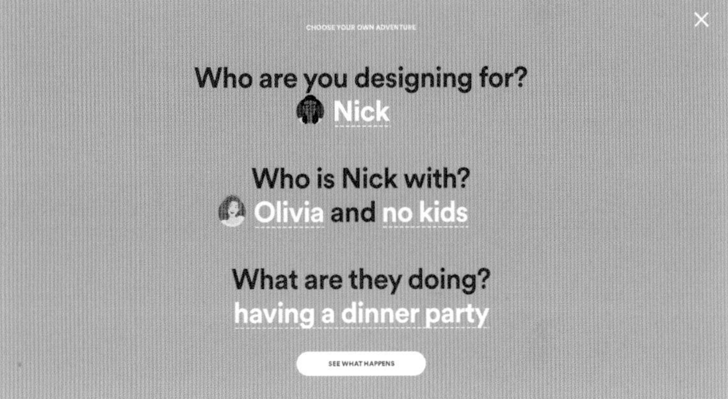

We developed a conversational interface for Spotify's internal research tool, providing actionable insights in under ten seconds.

25. Diverse teams create better solutions.

Design is run by white men. To be exact, 76 percent of people who design for the web are white, and 58 percent of them are men. That obviously is not representative of our society and leads to bias issues.

- Studies have shown that diverse teams, with varied experiences and backgrounds, actually find superior solutions to problems.
- Diversity also positively impacts financial performance, with diverse companies outperforming peers.
- It's also more likely that teams with varied perspectives challenge norms, avoid stereotyping, and reduce biases.
- And all this matters because digital tools, such as voice assistants with female voices, can reflect gender biases, resulting in a limited and stereotyped digital environment.
- As UX designers, our role is vital. By addressing our biases and ensuring inclusivity in our UX teams, we create a win-win for everyone.

26. Context matters more than screen size.

Mobile design goes beyond just making things look good on various screens. Each device, with its unique context, requires a design approach that's mindful of the user's experience (see Principle 84).

- Designing for devices is as much about the "where" and "how" as the "what."
- Mobile isn't just about fitting the screen; it's about on-the-go access, clear visuals under the sun, and easy thumb-scrolling.
- People shuffle gadgets based on their vibe: smartphones for commuting, desktops for work or tasks that require more precision, and tablets for cozy couch browsing.
- When, where, why, and how we access content needs to be considered well before we actually start designing anything, because when it comes to designing for multiple devices, there is no one-size-fits-all solution.
- When a system is designed for context of use rather than screen size, there is a higher chance that the interface will be more appropriate and feel more comfortable.

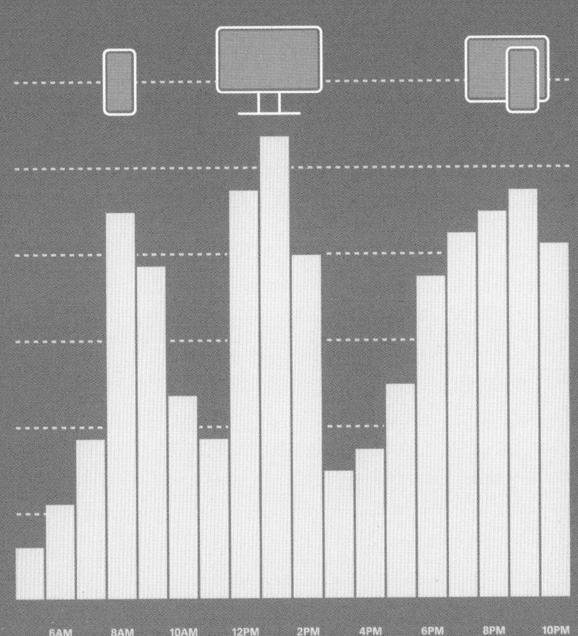
6AM
8AM
10AM
12PM
2PM
4PM
6PM
8PM
10PM

27. Design for clumsy handling.

Have you ever watched a toddler or a cat use a tablet? I was impressed when my baby boomer mother, new to computers, intuitively used her first iPad in 2012. She even changed the system language from English to Dutch by herself.

- For intuitive touch design, tappable areas should match the size of a human fingertip, similar to keyboard keys or remote control buttons.
- A study reveals the average human fingertip is 8 to 10 millimeters; that's why Apple and Android suggest a touch target size of 7 to 10 millimeters with 5 millimeters of separation.
- By adopting an oversized design approach, inspired by the simplicity of toddler toys which are made large for ease of use, we can ensure greater accessibility and user-friendliness for a diverse range of users.
- In essence, regardless of what we are designing, if buttons are bigger, options are fewer, and contrast is higher by default, we can accommodate a larger spectrum of users without much effort, from kids and seniors to those with motor or vision challenges, and yes, even cats.

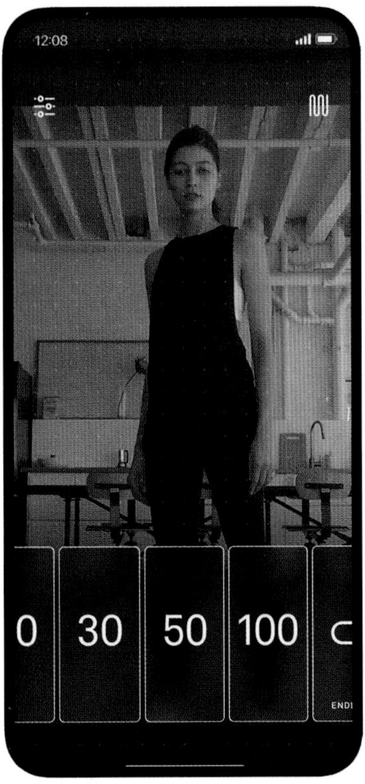

x100, our iOS app, ensures easy rep tracking during workouts with large, user-friendly interactive elements for sweaty users

28. Match the real world.

When designing interfaces, emulating real-world interactions helps make them more intuitive. That's why users can instinctively trash items, group documents, or use apps like the compass and calculator without guidance.

- Designing with real-world interactions in mind leads to more intuitive user experiences because familiarity simplifies use (see Principle 62).
- Observing how people interact with physical objects offers deep insights for creating instinctive and user-friendly digital interfaces.
- It's about thoughtfully converting real-world actions into the digital realm to make interfaces familiar yet efficient.
- For example, physical cues that already exist in the real world, like color-coding or segmenting, can be translated into digital formats to make navigating instantly intuitive.
- Ultimately, leveraging real-world patterns in digital designs meets user expectations, ensuring a smooth interaction experience.

Wolff Olins's redesign of *USA Today*'s physical newspaper from 2012, and the final UI of the digital newspaper we worked on simultaneously.

29. Know when to break with convention.

In 2000, researcher Jakob Nielsen argued that users prefer familiar site designs, suggesting designers should standardize interfaces. However, sticking to conventions is not always the right approach. Here's why.

- While following conventions can be comforting due to familiarity, it can also lead to a lack of innovation and a repetitive user experience.
- Sometimes, to captivate users, we need to think outside the box, offering them unique yet meaningful interactions.
- Being different doesn't mean creating chaos; a well-crafted unique design can be both fresh and intuitive, making a lasting impression.
- Intentionally deviating from the norm can result in memorable and intuitive experiences (see Principle 9), provided it's done with a clear understanding of the standard.
- If we do manage to create something new that is still very intuitive to use, people will not only interact with it easily, but they'll probably remember it much more favorably as well.

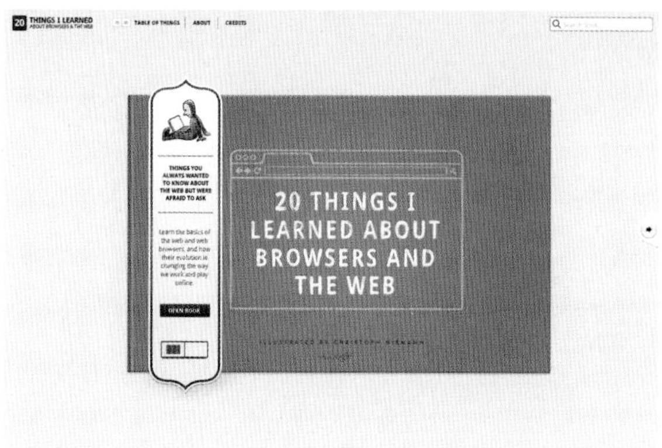

Key screens from the "20 Things I Learned about Browsers and the Web" interactive experience we worked on for Google that deliberately broke with the norm.

30. Persuade, don't coerce.

UX design can balance between supporting users and subtly manipulating for business gain. While our designs may look harmless, they risk exploiting users with psychological triggers.

- While UX design aims to champion users, it sometimes serves the hidden agendas of sales or marketing teams, incorporating subtle tactics to create addictive features.
- While gamification can reward users with badges, it can also be misused, extracting more from users than just their time and attention.
- Emotionally intelligent UX designers excel at understanding user behavior, but this insight can also be used manipulatively.
- Designers face a choice: create genuine goal-driven experiences or deliberately misguide users for selfish benefits (see Principle 5).
- If all UX designers would think about how every single product or feature they are working on might coerce people into doing something they didn't set out to do and raise the alarm right away, the internet would be a much more positive place.

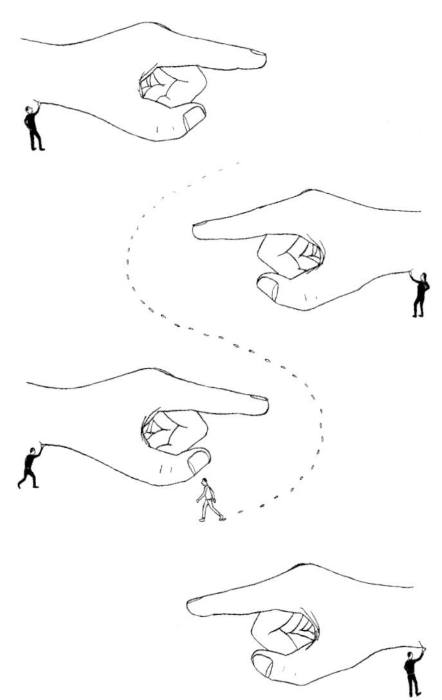

31. Design for passive attention.

Not every interface needs constant interaction to enhance user experience. While platforms like Instagram are active, smart home devices, such as lightbulbs, become decorative elements in our spaces. Their "always-on" displays blend utility with personal taste.

- The "Internet of Things" (a term credited to Peter T. Lewis in 1985) reshapes connectivity, emphasizing technology's role in enhancing our surroundings without persistent interaction demands.
- Platforms like Instagram rely on active user participation, while smart devices integrate subtly into our lives, offering utility without constant engagement.
- Smart devices like Google's Nest Hub, when introduced to our homes, don't merely convey information but become an expression of our taste in decor, navigating the fine line between utility and aesthetic.
- Designing for such devices should aim for seamless, respectful integration, enriching our spaces without infringing on personal tastes.
- An internet-connected device in the home has unique capabilities that an analog device doesn't. But we have to be very careful with how we use those capabilities and make sure we add to the environment rather than overtake it.

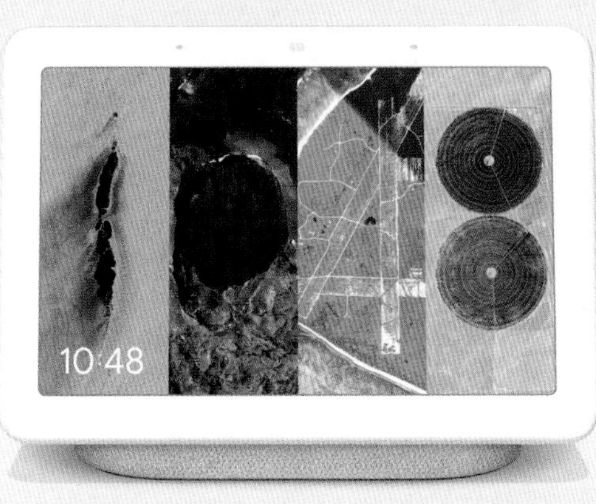

Diverse clock faces for the Google Nest Hub offer users choices to match their home decor preferences.

32. Know the purpose.

In the 1970s, German industrial designer Dieter Rams said, "Products fulfilling a purpose are like tools. They are neither decorative objects nor works of art. Their design should therefore be both neutral and restrained, to leave room for the user's self-expression."

- Users interact with digital products with specific goals, not focusing on the design.
- Every digital product, whether for shopping, searching, or content consumption, serves a distinct purpose.
- When people use a digital product they have a goal in mind, and they want to be able to achieve that goal as quickly as possible. If they can't, the design has failed.
- Optimal design functions seamlessly and aids users without drawing attention to itself.
- Digital products aren't art galleries—they're tools. They're a means to an end for the user on a mission.

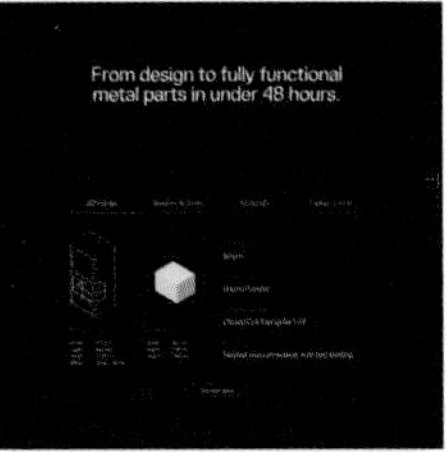

From design to fully functional metal parts in under 48 hours.

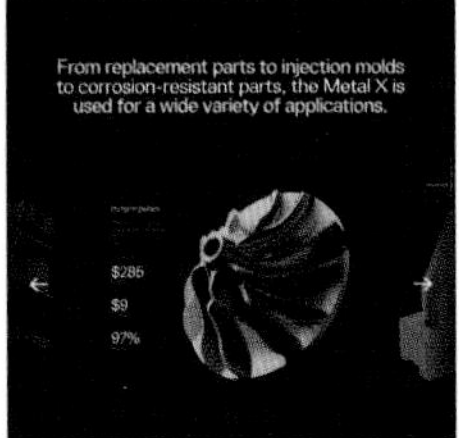

From replacement parts to injection molds to corrosion-resistant parts, the Metal X is used for a wide variety of applications.
$286
$9
97%

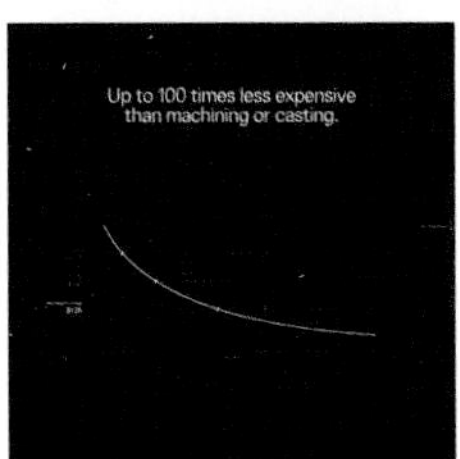

Up to 100 times less expensive than machining or casting.

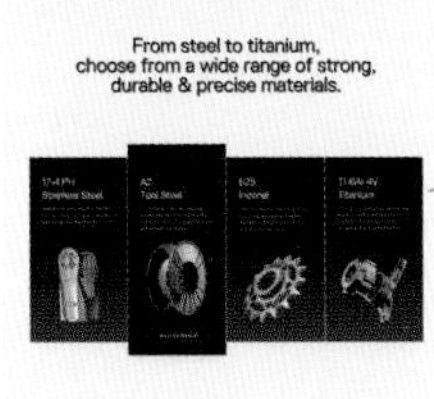

From steel to titanium, choose from a wide range of strong, durable & precise materials.

The enclosed build chamber & ultra-quiet motion system makes our printers perfectly at home on the factory floor.

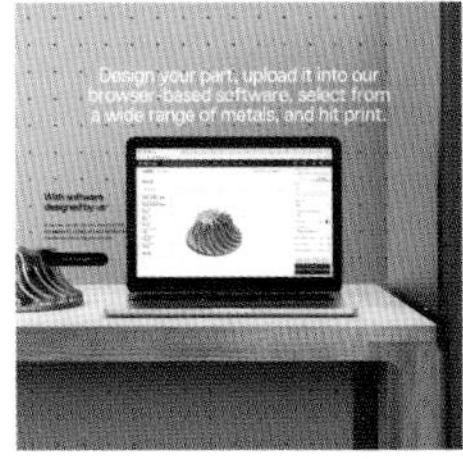

Design your part, upload it into our browser-based software, select from a wide range of metals, and hit print.

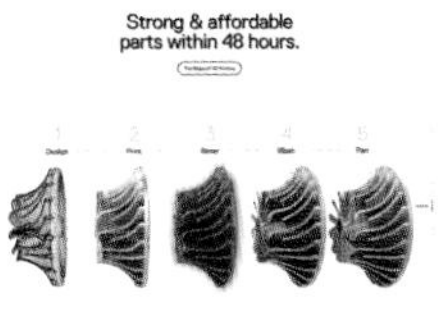

Strong & affordable parts within 48 hours.

Starting at $99,500

The Markforged website aimed to swiftly inform about transitioning to additive manufacturing, offering key factors and detailed insights.

33. Interrupt only when necessary.

Research from *Harvard Business Review* shows we're distracted every six to twelve minutes by non-urgent matters. *The New York Times* app notifies us of breaking news, Twitter (now known as X) tells us we have a new follower, Duolingo reminds us it's time to practice French.

- Research from UC Irvine shows that after a digital distraction, it takes us about twenty-five minutes to refocus on our original task.
- Post-interruption, we tend to detour to two other tasks—maybe answering an email or scrolling social media—before getting back on track.
- Given our high level of distraction when interrupted, we need to ensure that digital interruptions are relevant, arrive only when needed, and get delivered appropriately (see Principle 34).
- First consider whether the information is worth interrupting someone for. If yes, think about how to deliver that message. "YOUR HOUSE IS ON FIRE" versus "YOU JUST RECEIVED AN EMAIL" doesn't have the same level of importance in the real world. They shouldn't have the same level of importance on our devices either.

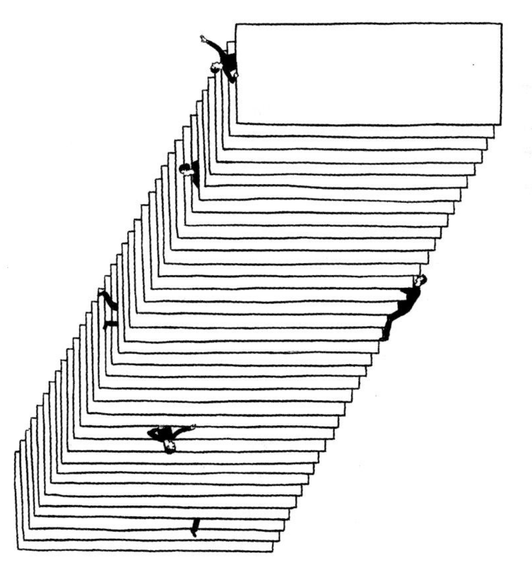

34. Make notifications valuable.

Microsoft's Clippy, known internally as "TFC" (with "C" meaning "clown" and "TF" meaning—well, you can probably guess what that meant), frequently interrupted users with unwanted hints. But people really hate being interrupted when they are focused on tasks (see Principle 33).

- However, notifications, when strategically used, enhance user experience. Imagine if there weren't any error messages informing us something was filled out incorrectly, or warnings right before we tried to delete something important.
- The best alerts assess both urgency and relevance, aligning with a user's current needs and priorities.
- Overloading users with alerts can lead to notification fatigue, making crucial alerts go unnoticed.
- The decision to send a notification should be carefully considered. It needs to be planned from the start. Ask yourself, "Is this genuinely beneficial for the user?" If unsure, it's best to refrain.
- If we treat the user's time as valuable and think of notifications as an assistant in potential moments of confusion, not as a sales tool, we're on the right track.

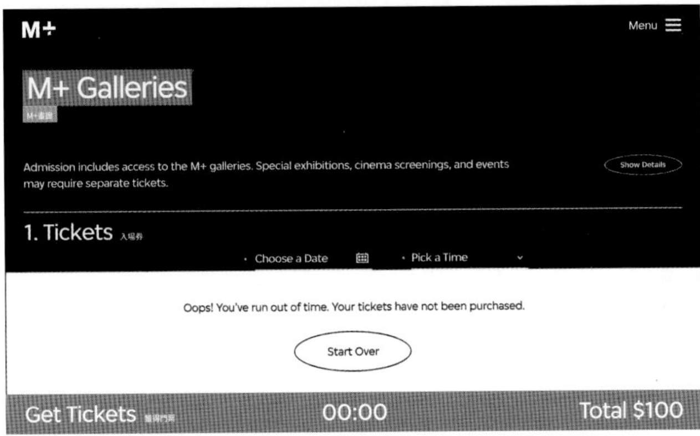

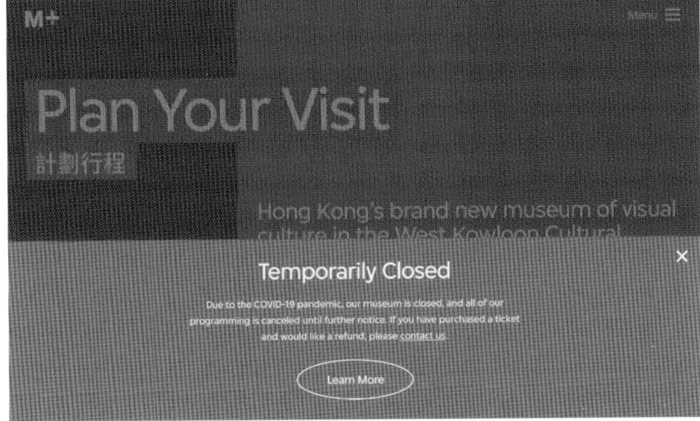

The M+ museum only sends useful notifications, minimizing interruptions for users.

35. Minimize form input.

Filling out any type of form is annoying. Yet, in our digital world, form-filling is an unavoidable means to communicate with computers. Whether it's for a purchase, a return, a query, or account creation, forms act as a bridge.

- Forms are essential, but an overload in form fields can deter users. Each added field can potentially push them away, so ensure every input truly matters (see Principle 11).
- But forms can also be engaging, even enjoyable. Our "One Shared House 2030" project transformed a form into an interactive, color-revealing, comparative-answer game, attaining our highest-ever conversion rate ever.
- However, always keep in mind that collecting data is a privilege; don't let it sit idle. Unused data risks breaches and can betray users' trust.
- Successful form design hinges on clarity, logical grouping, and ensuring a real need for data. Once gathered, it's crucial to have a clear plan for the data's use.
- Streamlined and thoughtful form design not only enhances user experience, but also ensures efficient data collection and fosters trust.

"One Shared House 2030's" gamelike form achieved record-high conversion rates, with 150,000 global participants sharing communal living preferences.

36. Little time, little design.

Minimalist design isn't just about looks; it can be strategic when time is limited. In our studio, using simple designs isn't just a style choice but a practical approach for quick execution (see Principle 11).

- There are many reasons why we might opt for a minimalist design. Minimalism isn't just an aesthetic; it's a strategic move when you're watching the clock and the budget.
- By stripping back to just the core, we find elegant solutions that balance innovation with user-friendliness, even on a tight schedule.
- Opting for a less complex design also expedites the entire design-to-launch process as fewer elements and features mean quicker design iterations and faster development.
- In other words, the fewer elements and features there are, the faster it can be designed and built. And that makes a huge difference when crunched for time.

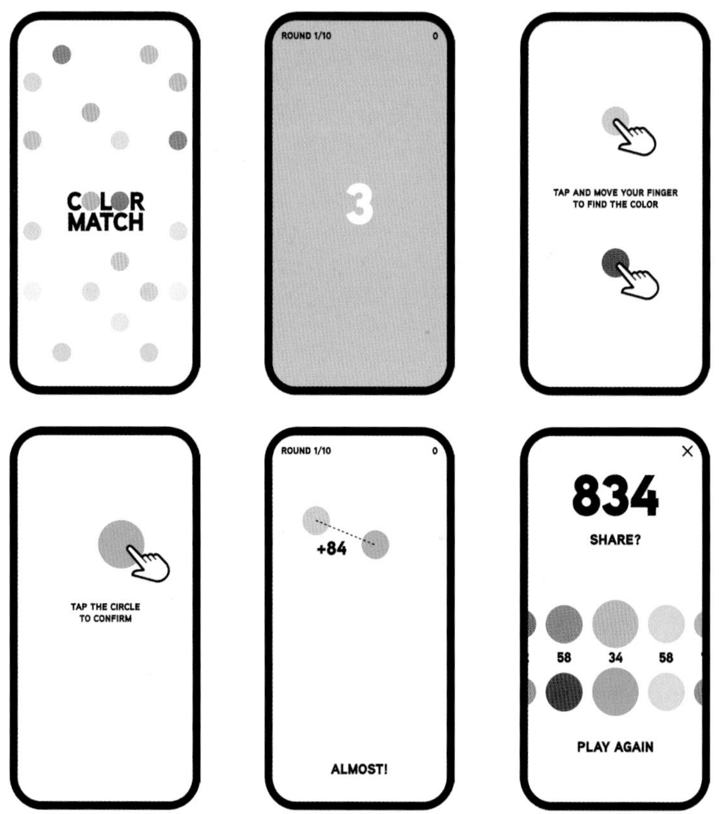

Our self-initiated Color Match iOS game was conceptualized to be designed and built within four weeks.

37. Rules are meant to be broken.

Usability and engagement can seem at odds. Traditional UX focuses on clear interfaces, but there's a charm in unconventional digital experiences that invite exploration, acting more like intriguing digital playgrounds than straightforward guides.

- UX design challenges us to blend established usability standards with experimental interfaces for engagement (see Principle 29).
- Intricate designs can transform user journeys into immersive experiences, capturing attention and sparking curiosity.
- Designers can craft interfaces that merge functionality with memorable experiences by balancing structure and exploration.
- Usability shouldn't always be the main consideration. If we don't need people to perform a specific task and just want to encourage them to play, high usability can actually stifle exploration.
- Merging guidelines with creative risks leads to digital spaces that seamlessly combine utility with delight; just be sure you are breaking the rules deliberately and not out of ignorance of the norm.

Shantell Martin's homepage breaks usability principles with a hidden "Play" feature, disrupting the experience but engaging those who discover it.

38. Choose the right client.

Never tolerate a bad client. It's better to eat ramen noodles for a month than to engage with a client who micromanages, limits access to their people, delays decisions, prioritizes politics over project goals, or disrespects your process.

- Always prioritize a healthy working relationship over enduring a difficult client; it's not worth the stress or complications.
- Effective collaborations hinge on mutual respect; choose your partnerships wisely and based on shared values.

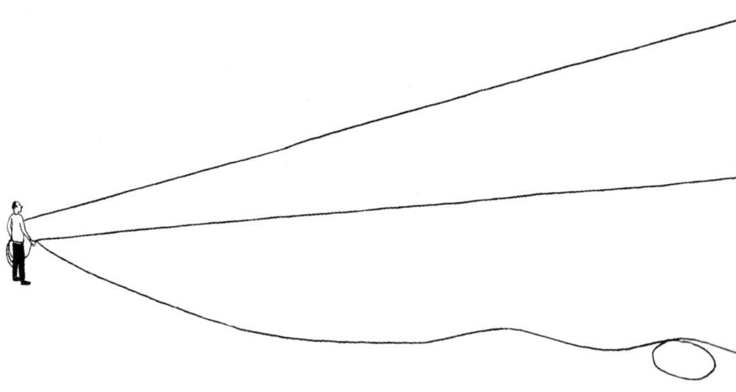

- First impressions matter. Keep an eye out for early warning signs during initial interactions as they often hint at future challenges.
- Even when presented with an ideal brand or product opportunity, evaluate their early behavior. This often predicts the overall project experience and ensures a good match beyond just the brand's or product's allure.
- Prioritizing the right client relationships safeguards your team's well-being and sets the stage for productive and respectful collaborations.

39. Be a good detective.

When we start a new design project, we admit to clients that while we may not be experts in their field, our strength is in guiding them through a design process that enhances user experience and their business.

- We begin by understanding the client's goals, whether rooted in research or intuition, ensuring we align with their vision (see Principle 56).
- Our process kicks off with comprehensive discussions, ensuring we grasp the client's perspective through purposeful meetings.
- These meetings encompass current design analysis, strategy brainstorming, role definitions, competitor insights, and establishing decision-makers.
- Following our talks, we create a guiding document—our north star—which steers every step of our project journey.
- Our detective approach means diving deep into client insights, ensuring a tailored design process that marries their expertise with our design expertise.

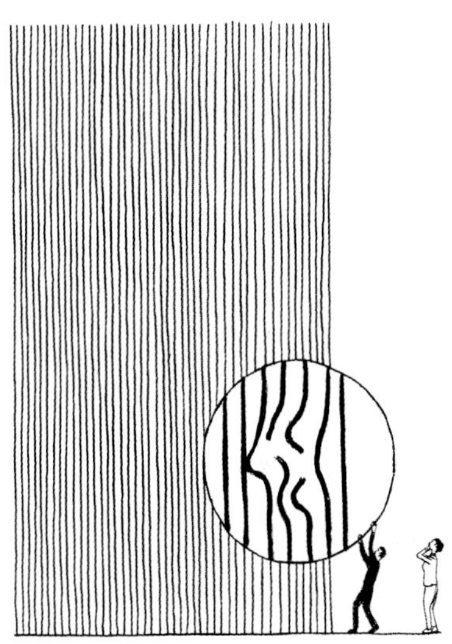

40. Gather requirements.

At the start of every project, we go through any existing documents (see Principle 56) and interview both the business stakeholders as well as the potential users. During these half-hour conversations, we ask broad questions to get in-depth answers.

- We use semistructured qualitative interviews, inspired by social sciences, to allow spontaneous topics to surface during conversations.
- Our main goal is to grasp the business perspective of stakeholders and deeply understand the end user's journey.
- Our discussions with clients zoom in on their experiences, challenges, and strategies they use to address issues.
- Post-interview, we compile a comprehensive report outlining key findings, underlying assumptions, and possible solutions, anchoring our subsequent research and design in authentic viewpoints.
- Through a meticulous requirements-gathering process, we blend client insights with user needs, ensuring a well-informed foundation for the project's direction.

41. Define the problem statement.

As UX designers, we both identify and solve problems. Design, unlike art, addresses human needs. As Donald Judd stated, "Design has to work, art does not." We must define the problem to create effective solutions.

- Setting boundaries can boost creativity, guiding us toward unconventional solutions.
- Project guidelines should be balanced; not overly restrictive nor too broad, pushing us beyond traditional thinking.
- With a clear goal, our ideas thrive within set limits, aligning all design decisions with the core challenge.
- True success is about discovering fresh and distinctive solutions, driven by careful constraints and a clear problem definition.
- A precise problem statement acts as the compass for design innovation, channeling creativity within structured bounds to address genuine user needs.

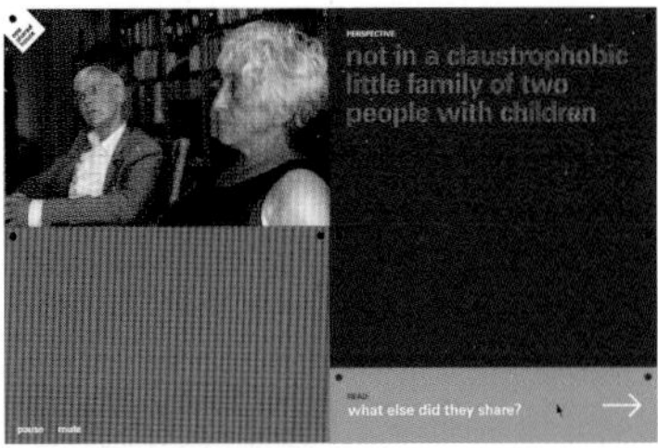

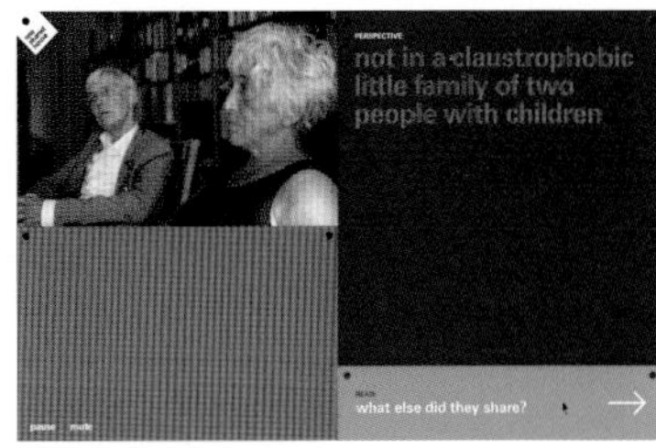

daily house dinner

official 8-page rental contract, 1984

what else did they share?

- Kitchen
- Rooftop
- Garden
- House Meetings
- Washing Machine
- Daily Dinners
- Bathrooms
- Communal / TV Room

They settled into their rooms, started having communal dinners and hanging out in the communal room, kitchen, and garden. The adults built a darkroom, a crafts corner, a guest room, and a painting studio.

They met up with groups from other communal homes, threw parties, hosted dinners, and got involved in city politics. They were hailed in the press as a shining example of communal living at its best.

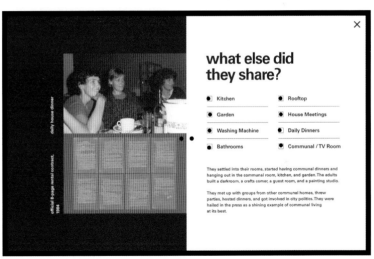

In "One Shared House," we explored video-to-text transitions, drawing inspiration from games like Carmen Sandiego and Zelda for seamless viewing and reading.

42. Find shortcuts.

Some projects have flexible launch dates based on features, while others have strict deadlines. If there's a tight deadline, we must ensure our concepts can be executed on time. So, we have to be cautious with our proposals (see Principle 44).

- Proper planning makes sure our designs are not only appropriate but also achievable within our given time frame.
- Early discussions and requirement-gathering allow us to identify and dodge potential hiccups, streamlining approvals.
- Understanding a project's limitations from the start helps us find clever shortcuts without compromising quality.
- Being aware of a project's constraints up front aids in efficient strategizing, ensuring speedy yet quality delivery.
- In tight timelines, proactive planning and recognizing boundaries enable designers to craft feasible yet innovative solutions, maximizing efficiency without sacrificing excellence.

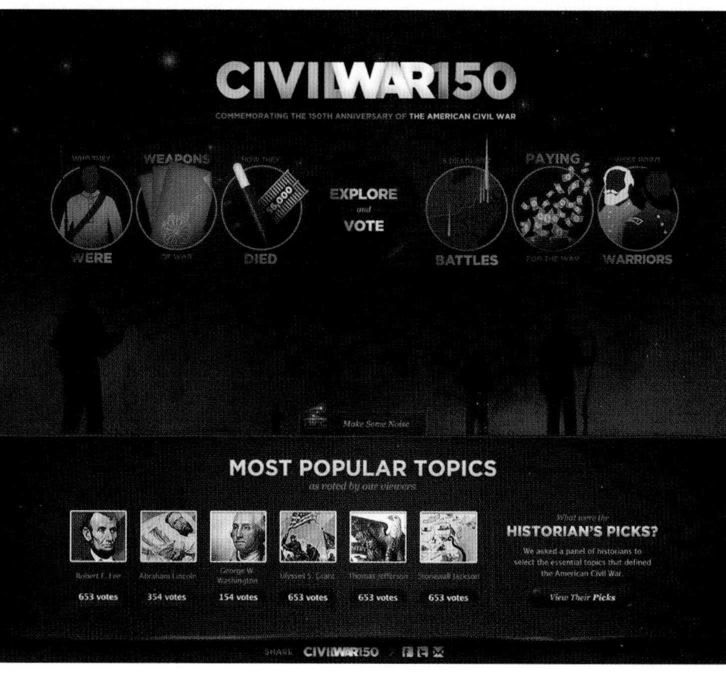

For the History Channel, we used nighttime silhouettes to creatively circumvent the need for extensive historical design research on Civil War uniforms.

43. Done is better than perfect.

Everything interactive on a website or app is a feature, like filtering or booking tickets. One of the toughest project decisions is distinguishing essential features from desirable but nonessential ones.

- The concept of "minimum viable product" (MVP), introduced by Frank Robinson in 2001, emphasizes launching with just the essential features.
- Launching products with only the bare essentials lets us quickly gauge user interactions and reactions.
- Initially, we prioritize crucial features for launch, while reserving additional desirable features for subsequent releases.
- Using a straightforward spreadsheet, we align features with business and user targets, evaluating them on business impact, user worth, and technical hurdles, ensuring a fast and targeted product rollout.
- Striking a balance between immediacy and perfection, focusing on core features for initial launch expedites user feedback and paves the way for iterative improvements in subsequent releases.

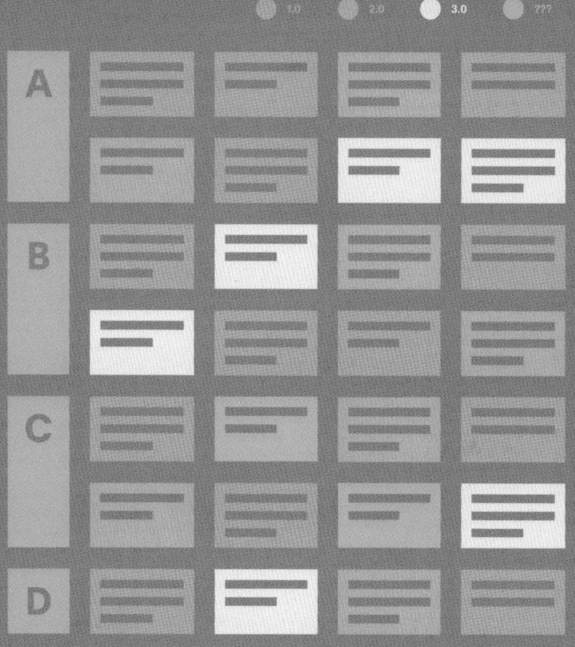
1.0
2.0
3.0
???
A
B
C
D

44. Underpromise and overdeliver.

Understanding which features to include from a business perspective is quite easy, as that requires conversations with only the business stakeholders. But figuring out which features should be included for the users is a little trickier.

- It's not as simple as only including the bare necessities for the launch (see Principle 43). It's also important to include some features that the user isn't expecting and will be positively surprised by.
- The Kano Model by Noriaki Kano offers a strategic approach to prioritize features, ensuring a mix that boosts customer satisfaction and loyalty.
- Regular evaluations help keep the balance between must-have features and those that surprise and delight users.
- As tech advances, user expectations grow. To keep up, it's vital to introduce fresh, impressive features periodically to reignite user excitement.
- Balancing core functionalities with unexpected, delightful features, driven by user insights and business needs, ensures a product that not only meets but exceeds user expectations, fostering long-term engagement and trust.

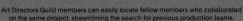

Art Directors Guild members can easily locate fellow members who collaborated on the same project, streamlining the search for previous production teams.

45. Introduce complexity only when necessary.

The biggest discussions in any project are always about the feature set—what will users actually be able to do in the final product? Most of the time, stakeholders get stuck on a cool idea without asking if it's essential in helping the user achieve their goal.

- "Occam's razor," a principle from William of Ockham, is all about simplicity, removing what's not needed and ensuring every item has a purpose (see Principle 11).
- The goal is to clear the path for users, trimming away any distracting or unnecessary content, and giving them the best experience without the clutter.
- Sticking to simplicity ensures users have a smoother experience, and helps keep projects on track, both time-wise and budget-wise.
- We often face a flood of feature requests, especially in big projects. But it's essential to remember that adding more doesn't always mean better.
- However, Occam's razor is not an example of simplicity for simplicity's sake. It is used to cut through the clutter to find the best solution without compromising the overall function. By shaving away complexity, features will have more clarity and impact, allowing people to use the product more efficiently.

SCENIC ART: PAINTING THROUGH TIME

SAMUEL MICHLAP

DANIELA V MEDEIROS

18 MODEL: YUKO HOUSTON

22 TRIBUTE TO JAROSLAV GEBR

6 THE CABINET OF DR. CALIGARI

30 COMIC-CON 2018: PREVIEW NIGHT

SCENIC, TITLE & GRAPHIC ARTISTS

JACKIE'S DESIGN. CREATING THE WHITE HOUSE IN PARIS.

FOLLOW ADG

For the Art Directors Guild website, complex feature requests were mitigated with the help of the Guild's executive director.

46. Some complexity cannot be reduced.

My MacBook Air is impressively lightweight, but the absence of USB, HDMI, and SD-card ports is a daily inconvenience. Apple's pursuit of simplicity has led to the need for separate dongles for basic connections, adding complexity to my experience.

- This is in direct violation of Tesler's law—from computer scientist Larry Tesler during his time at Xerox PARC—which argues that for any system there is a certain level of complexity that cannot be reduced.
- This idea suggests complexity just shifts; it doesn't vanish. Like a balloon, squeeze one end and the other expands.
- If we simplify user interactions, the complexity bubbles up on the development side, and vice versa.
- Instead of oversimplifying intricate functions, our aim is to make them *feel* more user-friendly and intuitive.
- Embracing Tesler's law means understanding that while we can optimize and streamline, we can't eliminate all complexities. The goal is to effectively distribute complexity to create a seamless, intuitive user experience without oversimplifying vital functionalities.

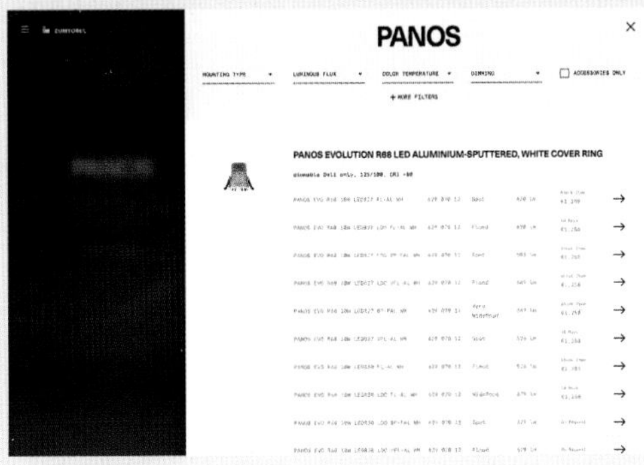

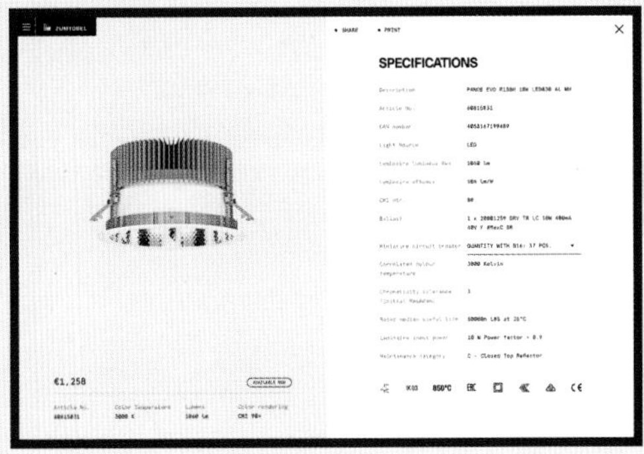

Zumtobel's website, dense with information, caters to lighting designers and architects, offering comprehensive data to support their decision-making process.

47. Imagine the user journey.

While the goal of a user might seem straightforward—like ordering a car service—the actual user experience encompasses myriad nuances that can shape the overall journey.

- Connecting a rider with a driver might seem simple, but in reality it's a maze of intricate scenarios.
- The "user journey" lets us step into the passenger's shoes, experiencing potential highs and lows firsthand.
- Mapping these journeys offers insights beyond mere data, giving everyone, from designers to business teams, a rich perspective of user experiences.
- Identifying issues helps us discern whether it's a design glitch or a business adjustment. By addressing both good and challenging moments, we elevate the overall user journey.
- Envisioning the complete user journey helps us anticipate and plan for various scenarios, ensuring we cater to both primary objectives and potential roadblocks. This holistic approach not only identifies pain points but also uncovers opportunities to surprise and delight users, enhancing the overall experience (see Principle 41).

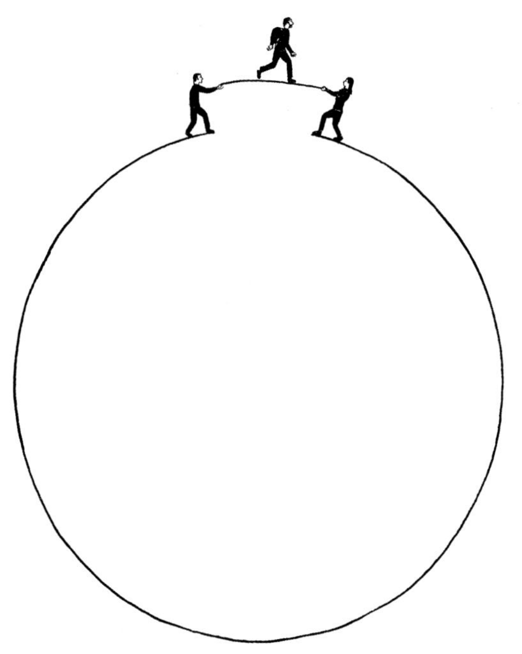

48. Create a user flow.

UX terminologies and concepts are not always the most straightforward. My students in particular are usually most confused between a "user journey" and a "user flow."

- Consider the user journey as a detailed road trip, capturing the entire experience, including the roadside views and pit stops, not just the drive itself (see Principle 47).
- The user flow, on the other hand, is like your car's GPS—it's a focused guide, highlighting steps within the interface.
- User flows are schematics that resemble flowcharts with boxes (actions) and diamond shapes (decision points) that display not only the ideal path but potential hiccups.
- The beauty of user flows? They provide a visual representation of all user pathways even before design begins, making it easily understandable for everyone, from designers to business leaders.
- User flows provide a step-by-step interface design road map, streamlining the process for a cohesive and intuitive user experience, allowing early identification of potential challenges.

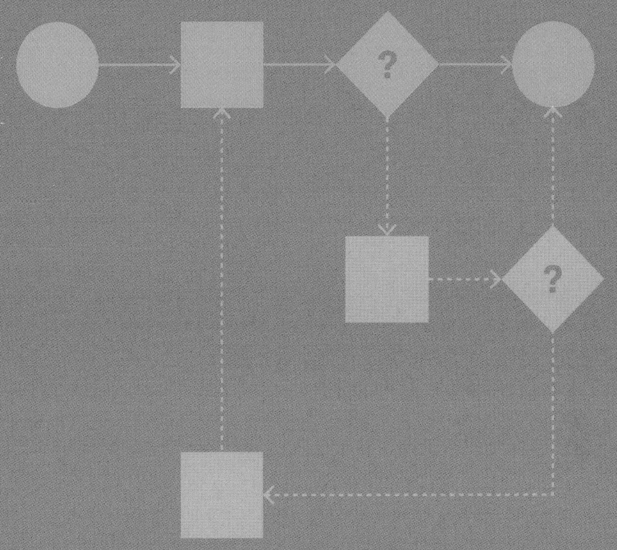

49. Remove barriers and obstacles.

Let's dive into some concrete ways of how to remove unnecessary friction from the user's path. A good "user flow" maps out one goal at a time, always has a clear starting point and end goal, and only looks at ways to shorten the path between those two specific points (see Principle 48).

- In the diagram, the happy path (what we want users to do) should always read in our natural reading direction, and the alternative paths (what users could also possibly do) should always fork upward or downward.
- This clear division allows for quick assessment of the efficiency of the main route and the complexity of alternate paths.
- Actions should be concise and clear, avoiding any jargon or overly detailed labels.
- After mapping the user flow, we assess each step for potential friction, tweaking paths for faster, smoother user experiences where possible.
- Efficient user flows streamline the primary user goal, eliminating needless steps. While alternative paths are distinguished, the focus remains on the main "happy path." Regular reassessments ensure minimal barriers and an optimized experience.

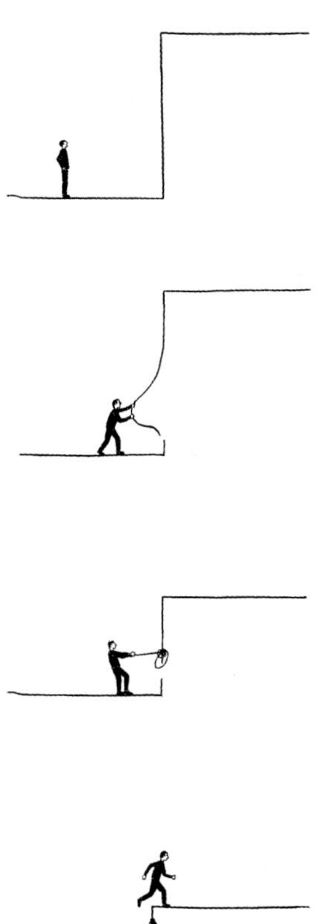

50. What isn't there matters.

Across all creative fields, what isn't there is just as important as what is there. In fashion, Coco Chanel advised, "Before you leave the house, look in the mirror and take one thing off." In music, Miles Davis famously quipped, "It's not the notes you play, it's the notes you don't play."

- In UX, how we present or conceal features during an interaction also heavily shapes the user's journey.
- Keeping nonessential details hidden streamlines navigation, reducing distractions and aiding users in reaching their goals swiftly (see Principle 11).
- Enhancing usability means fewer errors and quicker task completions, but we must be strategic in what we tuck away to avoid confusing users.
- Sometimes, what we choose not to display is as impactful as what we do, highlighting truly important features by sidelining the less relevant ones.
- In essence, across disciplines, the art of omission—knowing what to exclude—plays a pivotal role in enhancing clarity, focus, and impact, underscoring the value of thoughtful restraint in design and beyond.

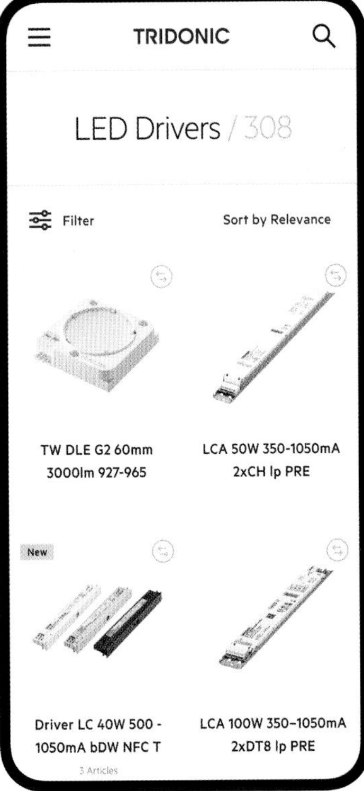

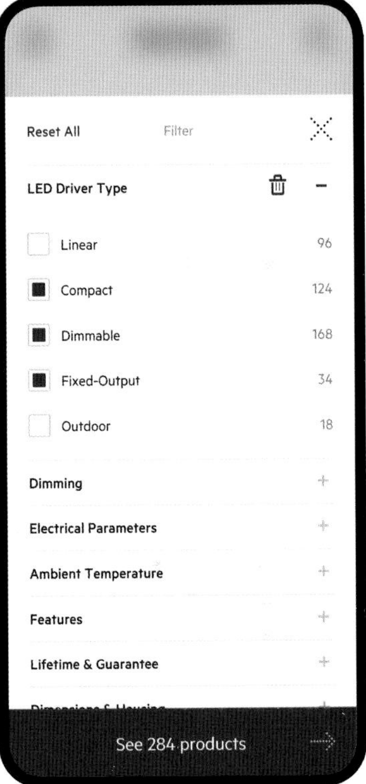

Tridonic's mobile interface exemplifies user-friendly design: filters are hidden by default, appearing when needed for a cleaner experience.

51. Pointing devices inform functionality.

Pointing devices refer to any kind of input that allows the user to control an interface. For desktop computers, that's commonly the mouse. For laptops, it's the touchpad, and for smartphones and tablets, it's our finger, and so on and so forth.

- In 1954, psychologist Paul Fitts introduced a model suggesting the time to hit a target increases with distance and decreases with size.
- Later, Stuart Card's study in HCI (or human-computer interaction) found that, based on Fitts's law, the mouse outperformed other pointing devices in speed and precision.
- Fitts's law now informs UX designs to optimize interface speed and avoid unnecessary user delays.
- To boost interface efficiency, it's best to have larger interactive elements, position sequential items close together, and ensure adequate spacing between them.
- Understanding pointing devices and principles like Fitts's law is crucial for designing interfaces that are responsive, efficient, and intuitive, emphasizing the symbiotic relationship between hardware inputs and software design (see Principle 84).

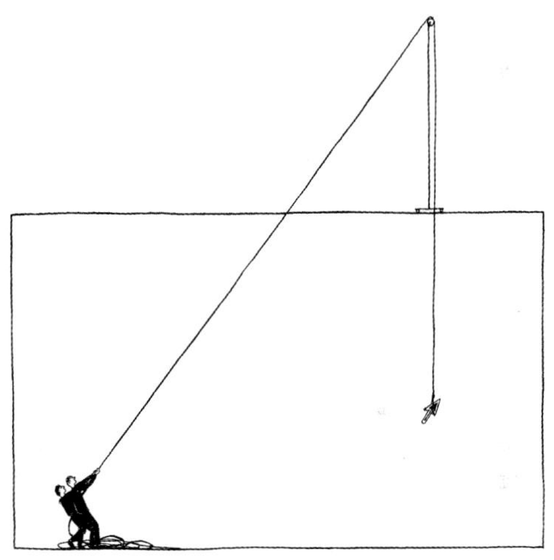

52. Design cannot be fully objective.

In 1972, at the Stedelijk Museum in Amsterdam, designers Wim Crouwel and Jan van Toorn debated objectivity versus subjectivity in design. Crouwel favored objective, rational design, while Van Toorn believed subjective personal expression was more impactful.

- Since then, graphic design has found its balance between rationality and personal expression, but the debate lingers in UX design.
- While we often chase objectivity in UX design, aiming for research to guide an unbiased approach, it's important to understand that this research is not scientific.

- Flawed research methods, like leading questions and biased usability testing, often over emphasize positive outcomes.
- While research can reduce personal bias, it doesn't ensure absolute objective design; human interpretation inevitably introduces bias (see Principle 53).
- Our strength as designers lies in balancing evidence with intuition, tapping into our unique human experiences and perspectives.
- Ultimately, while objective data is valuable, design thrives when it harmoniously blends rationality with personal touch, reflecting both empirical insights and the designer's intuition.

53. Most of the science in design is bullshit.

Can good design be reliably measured or assured? The short answer is kind of, but not really. And that's not something that businesses, which are seeking a palpable, demonstrable ROI, like to hear.

- Designers sometimes use misleading research techniques to obtain approval, exploiting business reverence for hard numbers.
- Even though research is crucial for understanding end users, setting focus, and validating decisions, it's important to understand that it is not an exact science.
- Design research is a subjective discovery process, seeking to expand understanding, not to produce quantifiable results (see Principle 52).
- Framing design as a strict science—which implies that it could be reproduced by whoever has access to the exact same data—undervalues the unique and intuitive journey designers undertake to create impactful experiences.
- In essence, while design incorporates elements of science, its power lies in the blend of intuition and experience, emphasizing the irreplaceable value of a designer's unique perspective and journey.

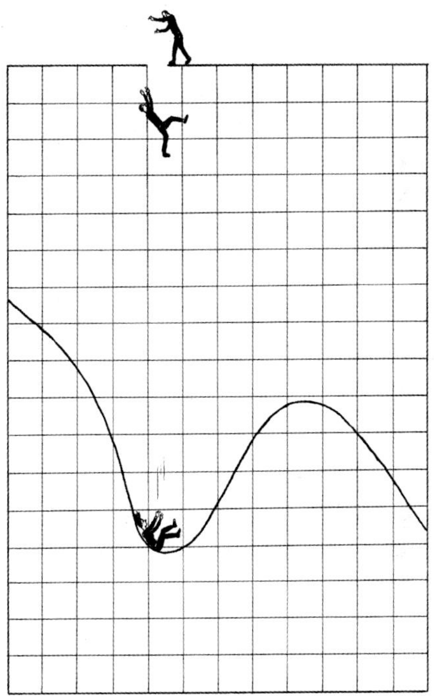

54. Do just enough research.

The extent of research depends on the project. Doing none risks missing the core problem, while excessively testing every detail can be time-consuming and stifle intuitive design choices.

- A project thrives on an equilibrium between methodical research and creative intuition.
- It's essential to validate assumptions about user pain points with actual interactions and feedback, bringing authenticity to solutions.
- However, allowing for intuitive design decisions, after establishing a foundation through precise research, ensures that the product doesn't just solve problems but also captivates and delights users in unexpected ways.
- The sweet spot in design is combining structured research with intuition, aiming to craft captivating digital experiences beyond just addressing challenges.
- In design, achieving the right balance between research and intuition is key to creating authentic and captivating digital experiences that address user needs and go beyond mere problem-solving.

55. Map the ecosystem.

Digital products can exist by themselves, but they are usually part of a larger ecosystem. Therefore, it's important to start by analyzing all of the company's current products and the connections between them.

- Mapping the ecosystem helps identify how a new product affects the whole setup and ensures strategy consistency across products.
- By analyzing user pathways, like from apps to websites, we get key insights into user behavior and how they use different products across different contexts and needs.
- This deep dive is a springboard for tasks like competitor analyses, creating user personas, and sketching out user journeys.
- Ecosystem mapping is crucial to understand how a new product fits within the larger context, ensuring consistency in strategy and providing valuable insights into user behavior and product coherence.
- In essence, ecosystem maps don't just provide a bird's-eye view; they highlight the coherence (or lack thereof) in a client's product strategy, providing a wake-up call for both designers and clients.

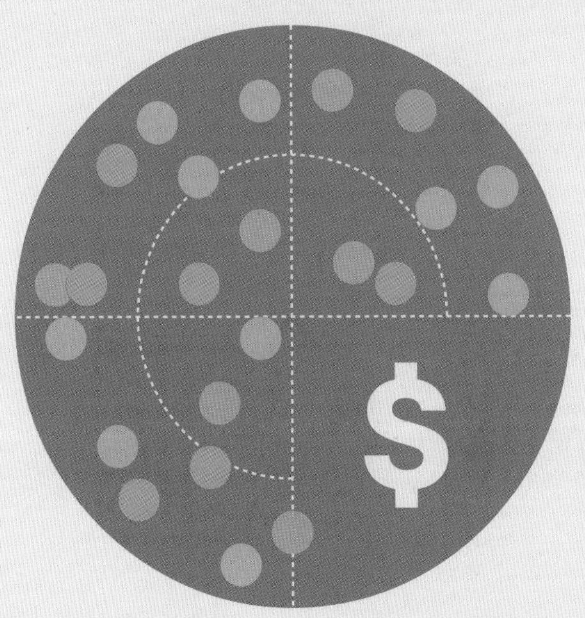

56. Look at the data.

Once the ecosystem has been mapped (see Principle 55), it's time to look at the existing data and cozy up to the client's marketing department.

- Data gives us valuable insights into customer behaviors and can hint at potential challenges or opportunities ahead.
- However, not every company has access to dependable data. Trustworthy data usually stems from products that have been in the market for several years. So new start-ups with recently launched products might not have a solid user base suitable for thorough investigation.
- When there's no data, looking at public feedback like reviews can offer unfiltered peeks into user sentiments and desires.
- But data alone isn't the key; it's a tool to understand user needs, setting the stage for our in-depth research.
- Data analysis offers insights into user behavior but should be seen as a tool to understand user needs and should be supplemented with comprehensive research for a more complete picture.

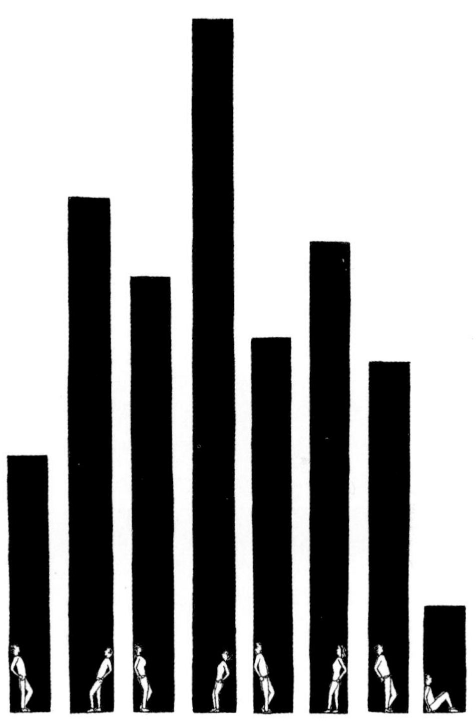

57. Not everything that counts can be counted.

William Bruce Cameron's 1963 text *Informal Sociology: A Casual Introduction to Sociological Thinking* contained the following passage: "It would be nice if all of the data which sociologists require could be enumerated because then we could run them through IBM machines and draw charts as the economists do. However, not everything that can be counted counts, and not everything that counts can be counted."

- Observational, ethnographic research in genuine user environments can reveal subtleties not discernible through quantitative measures.
- Watching users in their natural settings, like a café or a busy street, uncovers subtle behaviors and hurdles that numbers alone can't show.
- Through this kind of up-close research, we capture real stories, genuine needs, and unspoken frustrations.
- Those observations can then help tell a story that helps confirm our initial ideas and points us to truly user-focused solutions.
- By blending both hands-on observation and data analysis, we ensure our solutions meet users' needs and deeply resonate with their lived experiences.

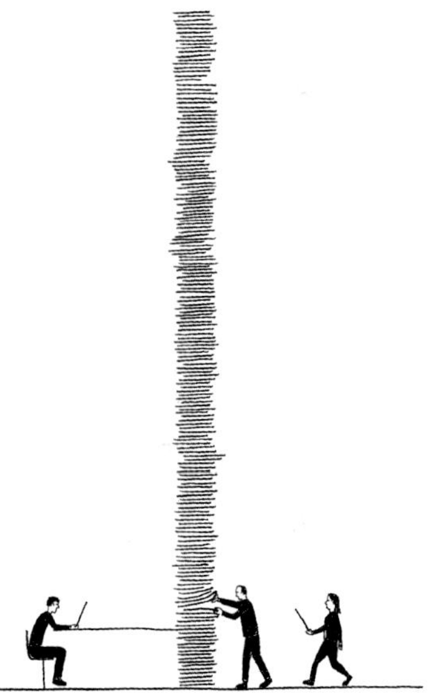

58. Test for statistical generalizability.

Quantitative research often tests an existing product's usability, like A/B tests comparing design layouts or measuring how many participants find specific information. The aim is to improve the current design's usability.

- Quantitative research uses hard numbers to clarify or challenge insights we've gained from observing or talking to users.
- This method typically relies on clear-cut questions like multiple-choice ones to make user feedback measurable.
- While these stats give our choices a solid footing, we shouldn't get too wrapped up in the numbers alone (see Principle 57).
- Always remember, while data guides us, it's our intuition and creativity that lead to truly standout designs.
- Quantitative research provides valuable insights through data and measurable feedback, but it's important to not only solely rely on numbers; let intuition and creativity complement quantitative findings to achieve stronger design outcomes.

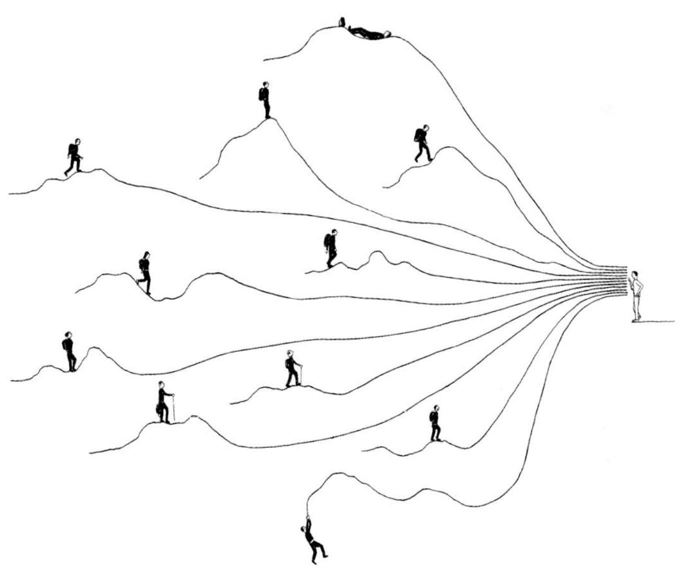

59. Don't base personas on assumptions.

The meticulous crafting of personas extends beyond simply combining characteristics; it delves into the essence of user behaviors and needs, ensuring every element is deeply rooted in researched reality.

- Derived from various data sources—ethnographic observations, interviews, and usage data, for example—personas embody more than just hypothetical users; they capture genuine user pains and needs.
- Think of them as reminders of the actual people behind our designs, helping us stay rooted in reality and not just our own assumptions (see Principle 1).
- By bringing personas into the conversation, we're reminding everyone that we're designing for real people, not just stats on a page.
- Well-researched personas provide a valuable perspective, but they should guide—not define—the design process.
- Personas should reflect real user behaviors and needs, keeping design grounded in reality and actual user research. Personas serve as a reminder that we design for actual people, not assumptions, and should guide rather than dictate the design process.

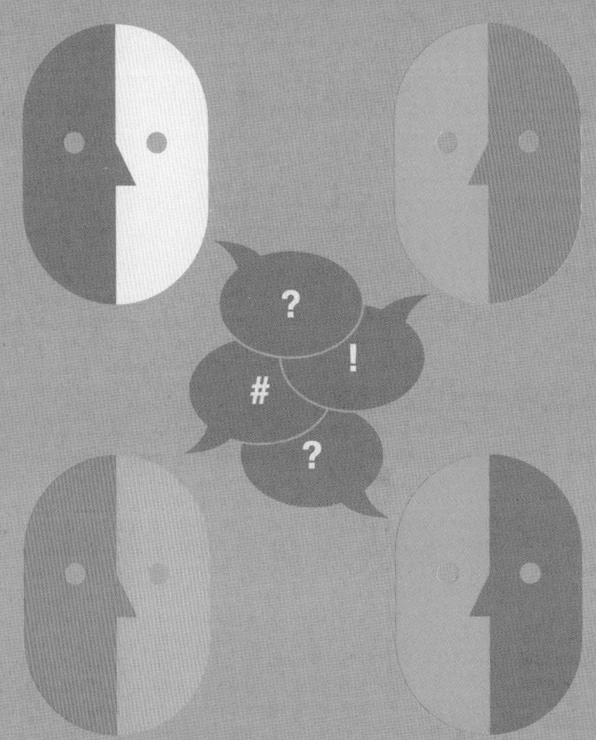

60. Keep your enemies close.

Whatever product or idea we come up with, it's very likely that someone else has already created something similar. Unless it's totally outlandish, it's almost impossible to create something that doesn't already have at least one, if not multiple, parallels.

- Analyzing competitors gives us a clear picture of the landscape: what's out there and where there's room for innovation.
- It's not just about mimicking what's already been done but understanding it to find our unique edge.
- While getting insights from others in the field is vital, we must be wary of only making incremental changes and not groundbreaking innovations (see Principle 41).
- Knowing the competition sets our bearings, but true differentiation comes from our unique design instincts and insights.
- Analyzing competitors provides a landscape overview and reveals innovation opportunities so we can find our unique edge. While competition insights are valuable, aim for groundbreaking innovation through your design instincts and insights.

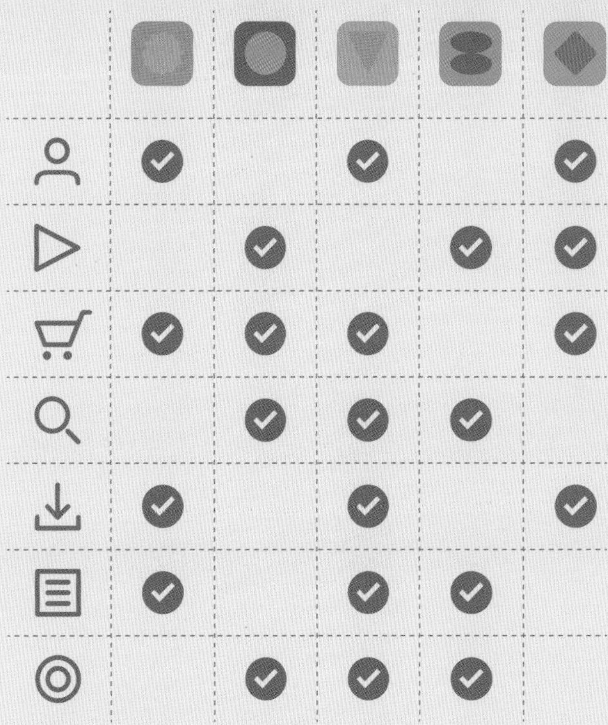

61. Learn from bad examples.

Products with usability issues offer valuable insights. That's why examining competitors through a heuristic analysis of their entire flow can be beneficial. While usability assesses a design's user-friendliness, heuristic audits evaluate the usability of an entire flow before designing.

- Instead of just spotting what works, we're zeroing in on what doesn't, collecting a list of design "don'ts" for future projects.

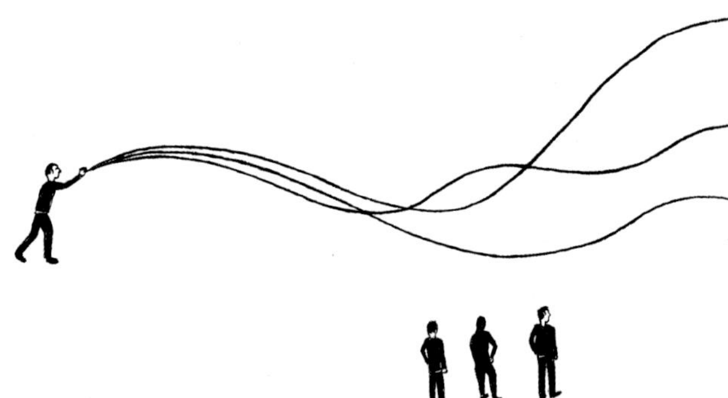

- We rank usability issues, from minor design hiccups to big roadblocks, giving us a clear action plan moving forward.
- Keeping a well-documented record is like having a design road map, and ensures we don't repeat past or others' mistakes.
- Because by learning from others' missteps, we're not only improving our designs but setting the stage for smoother user experiences.
- In essence, heuristic audits of competitor flows allow us to gather insights about what doesn't work while avoiding repeating mistakes and improving designs for smoother user experiences.

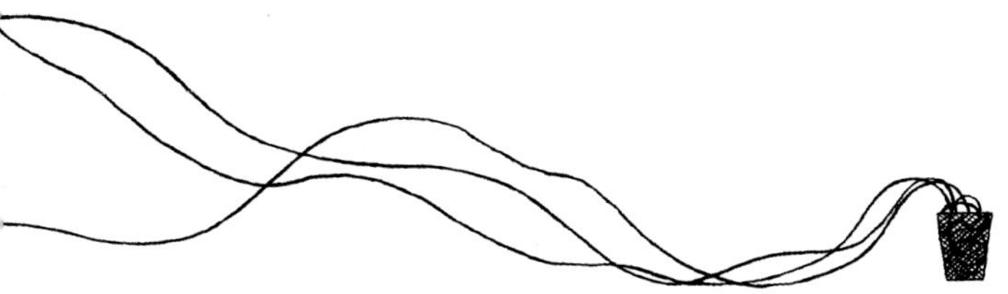

62. Make expectations work in your favor.

In 1943, Scottish psychologist Kenneth Craik proposed that people carry in their minds a small-scale model of how the world works, which they use to anticipate events and form explanations.

- We all have our own way of seeing the world, built from our life experiences and perceptions, which help us make sense of new information.
- Getting into a user's head is tricky. We can't just lean on our own perceptions. We need to recognize the gap between what they say and do.
- Techniques like card sorting give us a peek into how users mentally structure their world, showing us their unique take on both digital and physical spaces.
- To design something truly intuitive, we need to grasp how users think, sort, and interact with everything around them.
- Understanding users requires diving into their mental models, recognizing the nuances in their perceptions, and employing tools to capture their unique worldview, ensuring our designs align with their intuitive interactions.

63. Uncover consensus and ambiguity.

A card sort is a research method that allows us to uncover people's existing mental models to help design or evaluate the information architecture of a site.

- Card sorting is all about turning concepts into physical cards and watching people organize them in ways that resonate with their thinking.
- Before diving in, we need a strategy: Who's participating? Solo or group sessions? What's our end goal?
- This hands-on approach lets users show us their unique mental maps, giving designers a front-row seat to their cognitive world (see Principle 62).
- Listening to users' thought processes during sorting provides insights, helps us break free from our assumptions, and allows us to better align with users' expectations.
- In short, if we listen to a potential user's thought processes during sorting, we will better understand their cognitive world, breaking us free from our own assumptions and letting us better align with their expectations.

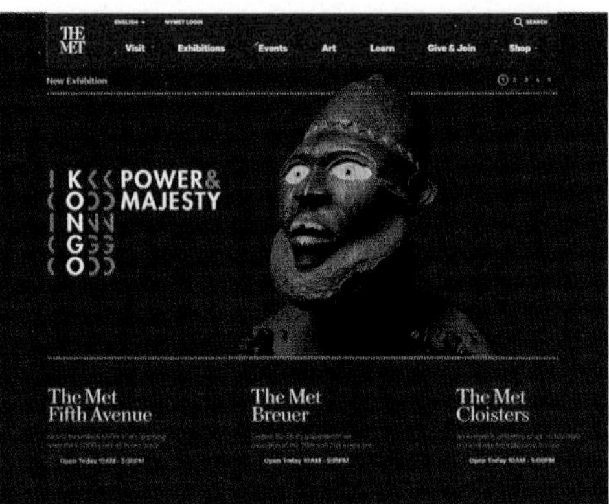

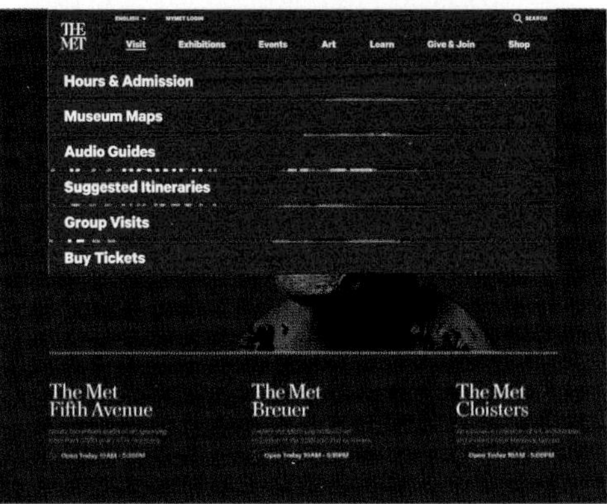

Met Museum's navigation is user-tested, stemming from on-floor card-sorting exercises with real visitors, ensuring a visitor-friendly experience.

64. Brainstorm efficiently.

Before the term "brainstorming" was recontextualized by advertising executive Alex Osborn in his 1948 book *Your Creative Power,* brainstorming meant you were having a sudden mental disturbance. That's why they almost called the method "thought-showering."

- Brainstorms can easily become time-wasters if attendees aren't prepared. Showing up with initial ideas is key. So, think by yourself for at least an hour first.

- A set brainstorming period, enriched by individual prep, allows collective ideation to flourish and interweave.
- Don't just talk—sketch! Drawing during discussions boosts creativity by activating visual areas of the brain.
- In other words, streamline the generated ideas, refine them independently, and collaborate on final decisions to ensure tangible next steps.
- Efficient brainstorming involves preparation, structured sessions, visual thinking, and collaborative refinement for actionable outcomes.

65. Build consensus.

If you ask a hundred different studios about their process for showing their designs to a client, you'll get a hundred different responses.

- While some advocate involving clients early in brainstorming or waiting until the final UI stage, effective buy-in often lies in between.
- Clear communication of the design process, pinpointing when and why we need client feedback, is crucial.

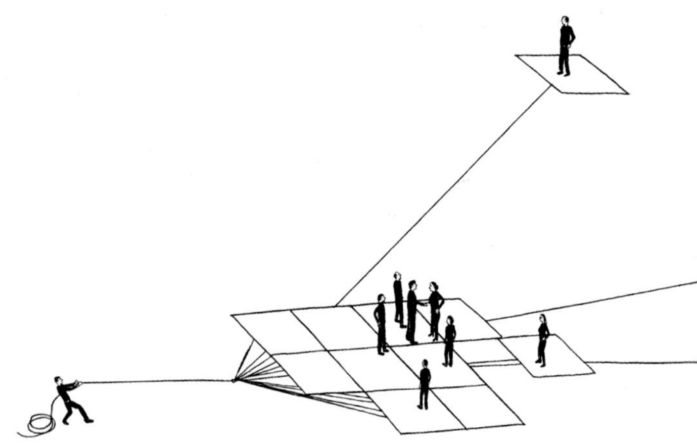

- Presenting high-risk deliverables, like the information architecture and key UI screens, early on fosters trust and smoothens project progression.
- Introducing brand elements during initial reviews aids client visualization and often eases approvals at the wireframe stage, streamlining production (see Principle 72).
- In essence, building consensus with clients involves clear communication, early involvement, presenting key deliverables, and introducing brand elements strategically throughout the design process.

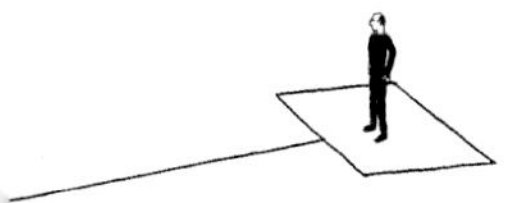

66. Learn from real-world navigation.

Observing real-world navigation, like the intricate yet user-friendly pathways of the Tokyo subway or the culturally resonant parking indicators at Amsterdam's Schiphol Airport, illuminates the fusion of practicality and innovative design.

- Observing physical navigation systems, like in daily commutes, offers invaluable insights applicable to digital design.
- Tokyo's subway, with its color-coded routes and clear diagrams, showcases the effectiveness of simple visual cues in user navigation.
- Schiphol Airport uses cultural icons in parking signs, highlighting how local elements can enhance user experience and memorability.
- Poor real-world navigation emphasizes the importance of intuitive digital systems that guide users seamlessly, reducing potential frustrations.
- To wrap up, any time you are actively observing real-world navigation, you'll be provided with insights for creating effective and resonant digital navigational systems.

67. Build a logical structure.

Whenever we talk about structure in UX design, what we're really talking about is information architecture (IA), a term that was first coined by architect and TED conference founder Richard Saul Wurman, in 1976.

- IA delves into a system's foundational structure, focusing on organization and functionality rather than visuals.
- Drawing from diverse fields, IA results in crucial navigation tools like site maps, categorizations, and hierarchies (see Principle 68).
- A well-crafted IA ensures users can smoothly navigate, no matter their starting point, and also ensures the system is scalable.
- Its importance can't be understated: poor IA affects search engine rankings, and like a building's foundation, a digital product's success hinges on a robust IA.
- In short, information architecture is the foundation of a digital product's success, focusing on organization and functionality to create a scalable and user-friendly structure.

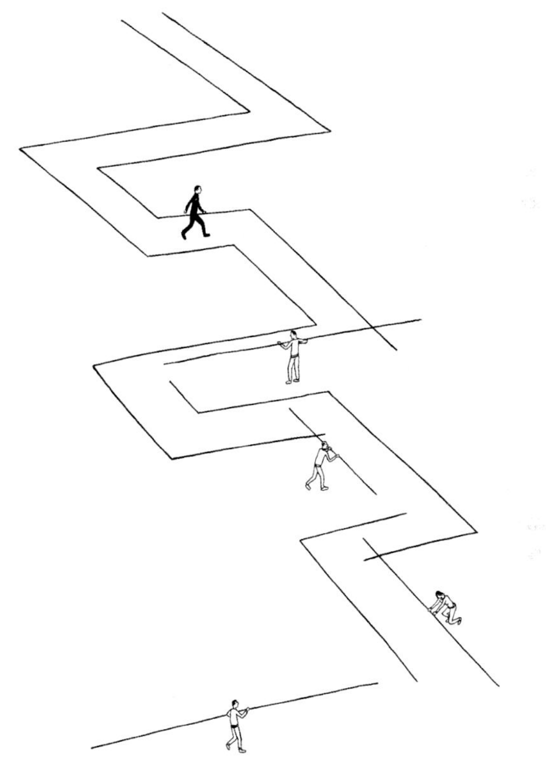

68. Visualize the relationship between pages.

All websites and apps are structured like Russian nesting dolls. As an example, let's take a marketplace-type website where you are trying to buy headphones.

- If a website is like nesting dolls: the homepage is the outermost doll, and as you navigate deeper, you encounter sub-categories, like electronics, then specific products, like headphones.
- Site maps lay out this structure visually, showing the hierarchy of pages and the user's potential journey through them.
- This structured flow should align with users' expectations, guiding them effortlessly from broad categories to specific items.
- A well-designed structure ensures users can easily navigate, backtrack, or discover related items, enhancing their experience and the ease of finding what they seek.
- Visual site maps illustrate the system's page hierarchy, ensuring a user-friendly journey from broad categories to specific items, enhancing the overall experience.

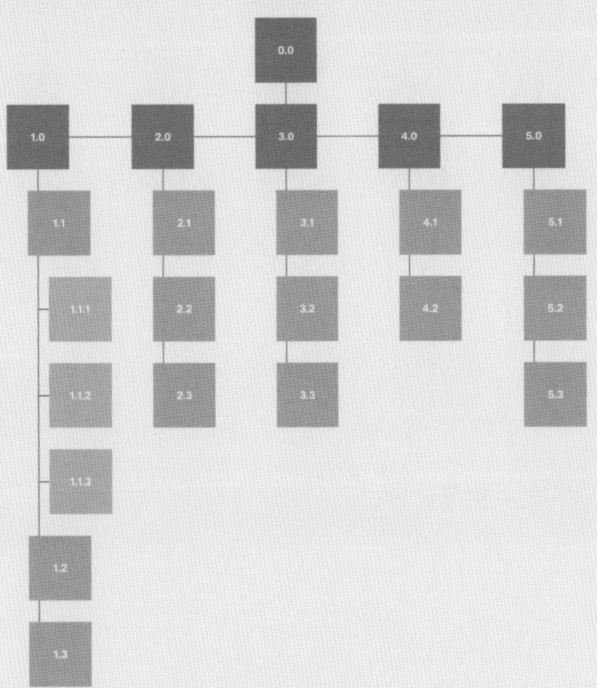
0.0
1.0
2.0
3.0
4.0
5.0
1.1
2.1
3.1
4.1
5.1
1.1.1
2.2
3.2
4.2
5.2
1.1.2
2.3
3.3
5.3
1.1.3
1.2
1.3

69. Don't get gimmicky with navigation.

Be careful. Overly experimental navigation can confuse users, making them uncertain about their location or next steps. If they can't find what they need, they'll leave.

- Stick to tried-and-true navigation conventions; they've become a universal language that users instantly recognize.
- Consistent navigation over the years ensures users feel at home, reducing confusion.
- It's key to make navigation not just visually intuitive but also inclusive, catering to diverse user needs.
- Reliable, user-friendly navigation acts as a safety net, offsetting other potential UX challenges by offering users a sense of familiarity.
- If you stick with well-known navigation methods that users are familiar with you'll avoid confusion and make it easier for them to find what they need, ultimately reducing any potential issues or drop-offs.

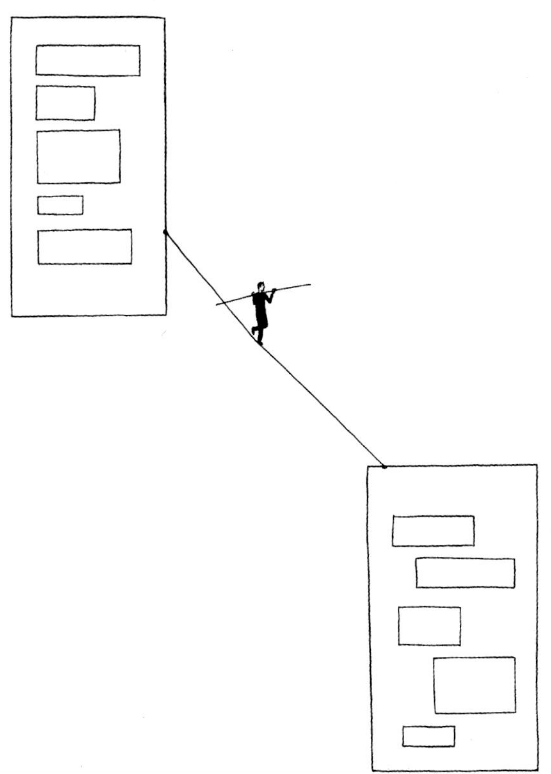

70. Yes, side doors matter.

Despite popular belief, the homepage isn't the most viewed or crucial part of user experience. Today, over half of a website's visitors initially land on pages other than the homepage.

- Users often access websites through search engines, social media, or direct links, bypassing the homepage entirely.
- Since users don't always start their journey on the homepage, every page needs to be designed as a potential first touchpoint.
- A homepage should set the tone and guide users, but the actual design focus should be on the frequently visited internal pages.
- The most visited sections or pages should receive the most design attention, ensuring a distinctive and memorable user experience for the majority of users.
- In short, identify and then focus on the most important entry points, not just the homepage. That way you will be able to ensure the most amount of design effort will go to the pages people will visit the most.

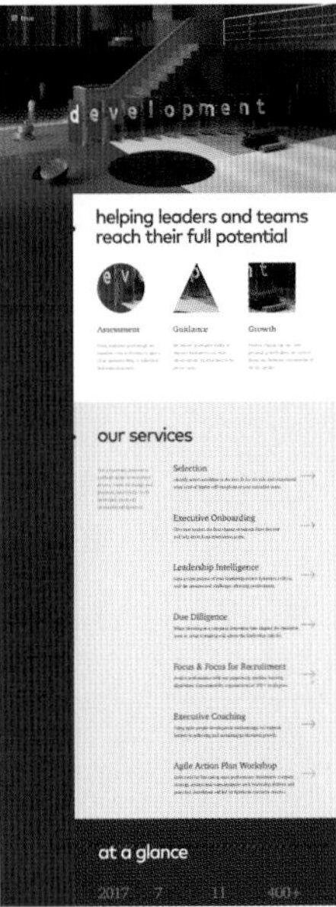

True's individual product landing pages match the homepage's impact, recognizing users may skip the homepage for a cohesive experience.

71. Priming before presenting.

In UX design, wireframes are the foundational blueprints showing interaction, content strategy, and information hierarchy. A well-navigated wireframe walkthrough creates a comprehensive understanding among stakeholders, ensuring everyone's on the same page.

- Wireframe presentations set the stage, introducing the basic blueprint of the future UI.
- Clear explanations ensure everyone, from any department, gets on the same page about the design journey (see Principle 65).
- Encouraging questions fosters collaboration and makes sure everyone feels included.
- By addressing potential confusion up front, the presentation aims for a unified vision and a jointly crafted final design.
- It's our job as UX designers to ensure the walkthrough is clear, and void of any industry-specific jargon or terminology that might confuse stakeholders.
- If your walkthrough is clear and inclusive, everyone will understand the design journey, which will encourage collaboration, setting the stage for a unified vision among stakeholders.

Lorem ipsum
dolor sit amet?

Lorem ipsum!

72. Move from low to high fidelity.

The fidelity of wireframes—the level of detail and realism—lies on a spectrum. On one end, there are loosely hand-sketched wireframes, and on the other extreme, there are detailed digital wireframes that visualize all content, visual hierarchy, and interactivity as close to the final UI as possible.

- Low-fidelity wireframes quickly capture layout concepts, emphasizing function over aesthetics.
- High-fidelity wireframes, close to the final look, need little explanation, making client feedback more intuitive.
- Detailed wireframes expedite both visual design and development phases.
- To save time in UI updates, we use high-fidelity wireframes for client feedback, offering a clearer glimpse of the final product (see Principle 65).
- When creating wireframes, consider moving from low to high fidelity along the spectrum to capture layout concepts efficiently, streamline client feedback, expedite visual design and development, and provide a clearer preview of the final product.

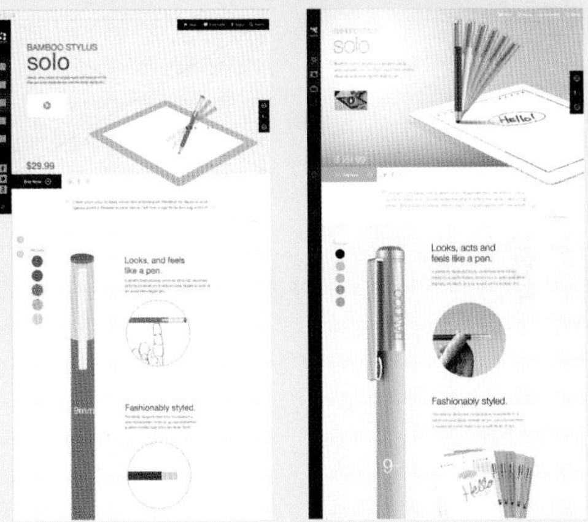

Utilizing closely resembling wireframes, we expedited the design phase and secured client approval before finalizing Wacom's product page UI.

73. Don't just illustrate, annotate.

Annotations explain in words how dynamic elements in a wireframe function. They're paired with numbered labels on the design, allowing easy cross-referencing for viewers.

- Developers, UI designers, and other team members refer to annotations to guide their tasks, while clients lean on them for feedback.
- Detailed annotations double-check our logic, ensuring we don't miss crucial details like error states or animations.
- Looking back on past projects, annotations capture the decision-making process, even if it's been ages since completion.
- The goal is to have our wireframes speak for themselves, answering any question without constantly pulling in the UX designer.
- When creating wireframes, don't just illustrate; use annotations to explain how elements function. Good annotations are a reference for team members, guide logic, provide historical context, and make wireframes self-explanatory.

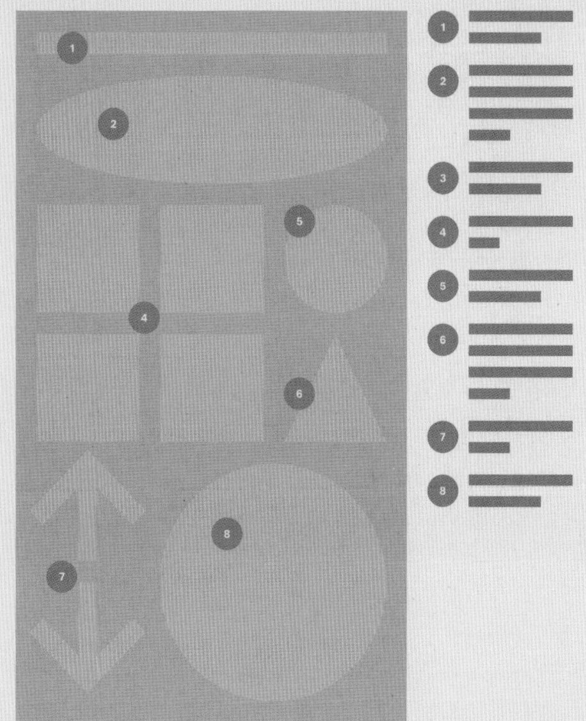
1
2
3
4
5
6
7
8

74. Interaction design is the brand.

If branding's job is to create a set of distinguishing features to promote awareness and recognizability of a product, then the UX and UI of the company's websites or apps are the most important vehicle toward influencing choice.

- Nearly half of people discover brands on social media, while a third head straight to the company's website.
- In our studio, we handle branding in three ways: building on strong existing brands, partnering with branding agencies for a fresh start, or modernizing old or nonexistent brands through interaction design.
- The twist today is that interaction design largely influences a brand's image, more than traditional graphic design or print media.
- A poor user experience can damage a well-crafted brand identity, and an unsuitable UI can quickly repel users (see Principle 8).
- In today's context, interaction design, more than graphic design, defines a brand, influencing how people discover and perceive it on websites and apps. It plays a pivotal role in building, refreshing, or modernizing brands, highlighting the importance of a seamless user experience in shaping brand identity.

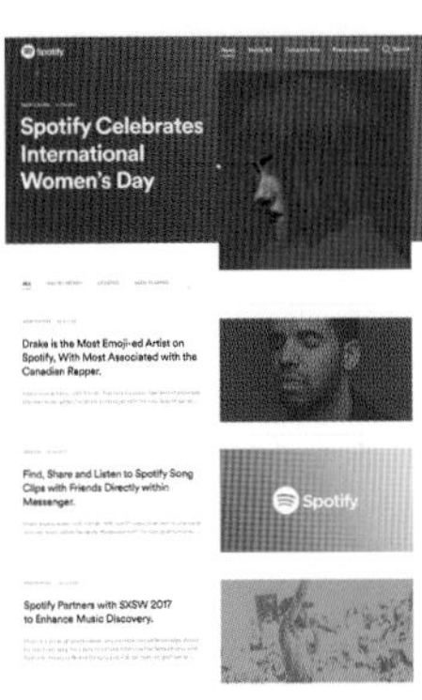

Key screens from our work with Spotify, Alpine Investors, and Markforged, each presenting unique branding creation challenges.

75. Bad typography leads to bad UX.

Just like color, shapes, and music can evoke different emotions, so can typography. A design can go from old-fashioned to modern to chic by simply swapping out the typeface, making type an incredibly important branding element of the UI.

- But in digital design, picking a typeface isn't just about evoking the right emotion; it's crucial for usability and accessibility due to the varied user contexts (see Principle 18).
- Screen typography differs from print; UI designers need a more cautious approach since screens come with unique challenges.
- On-screen text needs to be readable, scannable, and legible, emphasizing the importance of accessible design.
- A good rule of thumb: Keep text above sixteen points and limit lines to sixty to eighty characters to ensure clarity.
- In other words, typography in digital design is more than aesthetics; it plays a vital role in usability and accessibility. Choosing the right typeface is essential for readability and legibility, especially on screens, where unique challenges require a cautious approach.

76. So you think you can scroll.

Let's clear up a common UX misconception: Users do scroll. Despite widespread belief in the importance of placing content "above the fold," evidence shows users actually prefer smoothly scrolling through content rather than constantly clicking.

- Scrolling signals curiosity, wanting more; clicking typically suggests moving on.
- "Scrollytelling" combines storytelling with scrolling, revealing content and animations as users navigate and offering an immersive experience.
- This method transforms content into dynamic journeys, boosting engagement across diverse digital platforms, from articles to brand sites.
- But be cautious! While great scrollytelling enhances user control and engagement, poor executions, like "scrolljacking," can derail the experience with misaligned animations and stories.
- As UX designers, we need to clarify to our clients that users do scroll and often prefer it. While storytelling through scrolling can boost engagement, it's important to do it right to prevent any disruptions.

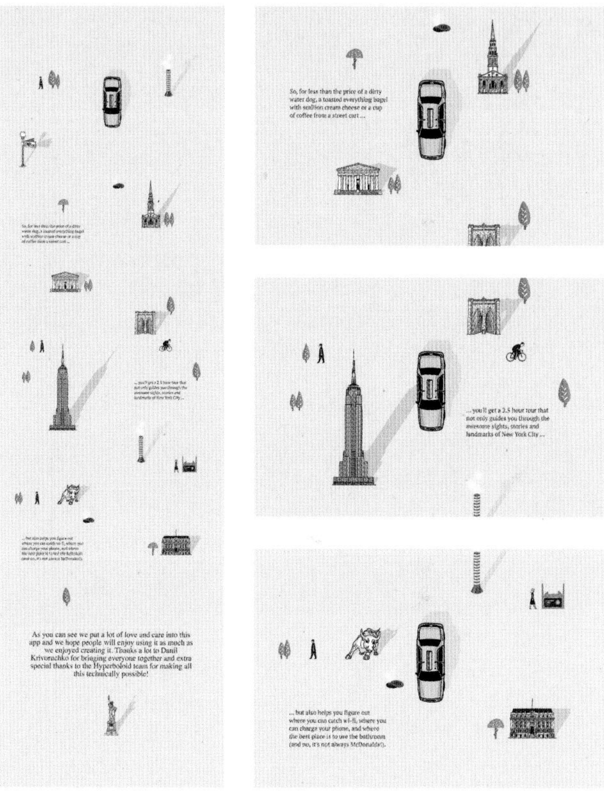

Our *UrbanWalks* app site used a NYC taxicab's top view to guide users. Scrolling controlled taxi speed, enhancing storytelling.

77. Animate responsibly.

The first use of functional animation in a digital interface was in 1985. Brad Myers's research on "percent-done progress indicators" demonstrated that visual updates on a computer's status make the wait more tolerable for users.

- This research gave birth to the progress bar and all other functional animations that followed.
- While decorative animations don't have a direct function, they can make interfaces pop and tell a story when done right; but if overdone, they can distract users.
- Even without a direct function, animations can add flair and uniqueness to the interface.
- However, be sure to always prioritize usability: Before adding any animation, ensure it enhances the user experience rather than hindering it.
- Simply put, functional animations, such as progress bars, improve user experience by offering visual guidance. While decorative animations can add style, they shouldn't divert users' attention. Usability should always come first when adding animations.

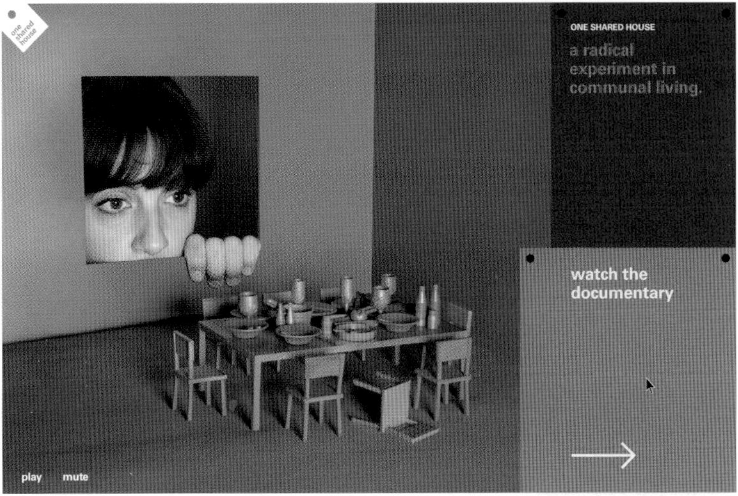

Our interactive documentary's homepage in Amsterdam tracks the mouse cursor. When "watch the documentary" is chosen, the pink chair falls.

78. Make data lovable.

Many people think of “data” and “data visualization” as just charts or statistics, which can seem boring or complex. Even though these visualizations aim to make big numbers more understandable, they can sometimes make things more confusing.

- Using visual metaphors is effective; use well-known symbols to help audiences understand complex topics like big data (see Principle 7).
- To make data relatable, weave a story around it, using the data as pillars to guide and enrich the user experience.
- It’s essential to remember that not every piece of data requires visualization. In today’s big data age, there’s a temptation to represent all data visually, which is not always the best solution.
- Always ensure the data you’re highlighting resonates with your audience; pointless data visuals are just background noise.
- Use visual metaphors and storytelling to make data relatable and engaging, but be selective in what data you choose to visualize to avoid overwhelming users.

We developed an interactive, user-generated story library for Porsche, visualizing thousands of owner stories in a geographical and chronological family tree that enhanced user immersion and community.

79. Dark mode rises.

Dark mode refers to a type of screen display that has light text on a dark background, also known as "negative polarity." Light mode, on the other hand, has dark text on a light background, which is "positive polarity."

- Developers often favor dark mode for its eye comfort in prolonged use and notable distinction of code against a dark backdrop, attributed to reduced blue light and enhanced readability.
- Light mode is generally favored for reading extended text by the rest of us, given our natural bias for dark text on light backgrounds—we are not nocturnal creatures after all.
- As a rule of thumb, we use dark mode for tasks in low light or for highlighting visuals, and light mode for in-depth reading in well-lit areas.
- But you can always offer both. Offering users the choice to toggle between modes ensures adaptability to diverse needs and situations.
- Provide both dark mode and light mode options to accommodate users' preferences and different use cases, offering enhanced readability in various lighting conditions.

Metamorphosis

One morning, when Gregor Samsa woke from troubled dreams, he found himself transformed in his bed into a horrible vermin. He lay on his armour-like back, and if he lifted his head a little he could see his brown belly, slightly domed and divided by arches into stiff sections. The bedding was hardly able to cover it and seemed ready to slide off any moment. His many legs, pitifully thin compared with the size of the rest of him, waved about helplessly as he looked.

“What’s happened to me?” he thought. It wasn’t a dream. His room, a proper human room although a little too small, lay peacefully between its four familiar walls. A collection of textile samples lay spread out on the table—Samsa was a travelling salesman —and above it there hung a picture that he had recently cut out of an illustrated

14

Metamorphosis

One morning, when Gregor Samsa woke from troubled dreams, he found himself transformed in his bed into a horrible vermin. He lay on his armour-like back, and if he lifted his head a little he could see his brown belly, slightly domed and divided by arches into stiff sections. The bedding was hardly able to cover it and seemed ready to slide off any moment. His many legs, pitifully thin compared with the size of the rest of him, waved about helplessly as he looked.

“What’s happened to me?” he thought. It wasn’t a dream. His room, a proper human room although a little too small, lay peacefully between its four familiar walls. A collection of textile samples lay spread out on the table—Samsa was a travelling salesman —and above it there hung a picture that he had recently cut out of an illustrated

14

Light mode often favors reading, while dark mode enhances image emphasis and visibility.

80. Never give total control.

The more flexible the interface, the more control the user has. But the more control the user has, the more complex the interface becomes (see Principle 46).

- User control should be tailored: general users need moderate options, while pros might need more advanced ones.
- Basic functions like undo or cancel are essential, but full customization is best saved for expert users.
- Finding the sweet spot means giving users enough tools without overwhelming them.
- Designers should focus on the audience's needs, ensuring tools aren't too complex or underused.
- Customization options in an interface should be balanced, offering essential functions for general users and providing advanced features for expert users without overwhelming anyone.

RYAN GROSSHEIM

ASSISTANT ART DIRECTOR - FILM

SEND EMAIL
IMDB PROFILE
WWW.RYANGROSSHEIM.COM
TUMBLR.RYANGROSSHEIM.COM
PDF RESUME

AGENT: DAN BROWN
AGENCY: BROWN LLC
AGENCY PHONE: 123-456-6788
AGENCY CELL: 123-456-6788
EMAIL AGENT

YOUR PROFILE IS SET TO **PUBLIC** CHANGE

CHANGE PASSWORD

Ryan Grossheim is a Production Designer & Art Director for film/television based in southern California. He also works as a scenic designer and concept artist for themed entertainment and theatre with clients including the San Diego Zoo.

SKILLS

Scenic Painting: Theatrical
Computer/Design: Adobe Illustrator
Computer/Design: Adobe InDesign
Computer/Design: Adobe Photoshop
Computer/Design: Vectorworks
Drafting/Models: Foamcore Models
Drafting/Models: Finish Models
Title/Graphics: Logo Design
Title/Graphics: Production Graphics
Computer/Design: AutoCAD (AutoDesk)
Computer/Design: SketchUp

EXPERIENCE

Extensive Experience in Design for Theatre and Themed Entertainment

MFA - Design & Technology - San Diego State Dept. of Theatre, Television and Film

Lorem ipsum dolor sit amet, consectetuer adipiscing elit. Aenean commodo ligula eget dolor. Aenean massa.

Mac and PC proficient

RECOGNITION

Emmy Award for *Hairspray Live!*
ADG Nomination for Hairspray Live!
Emmy Nomination for The Voice
ADG Nomination for The Voice

LOCATION EXPERIENCE

Los Angeles, Boston, Chicago

CREDITS

ADD CREDIT

MINDHUNTER

NETFLIX

MINDHUNTER
SEASON 1, 2
ASSISTANT ART DIRECTOR

THE GOOD PLACE
SEASON 1, 2
ASSISTANT ART DIRECTOR

Hairspray Live!

HAIRSPRAY LIVE!
ASSISTANT ART DIRECTOR

Art Directors Guild members can personalize their profile details and privacy but cannot alter the page's design.

81. Personalization is hit or miss.

If customization is about giving users control, then personalization is about giving that control to the system to make decisions about what it thinks the user wants based on previous behavior.

- Personalization walks a fine line between helpful suggestions and becoming too invasive.
- Recommendations are great for content discovery but can feel creepy if they're too on the nose or invasive if they miss the mark.
- Most people are okay with data use if they've shared it knowingly; therefore getting clear consent is key (see Principle 14).
- While using past behaviors can guide recommendations, users also value fresh, unexpected content, so it shouldn't feel like options are hidden from them.
- Personalization involves a balance between providing helpful suggestions based on user behavior and respecting user privacy and consent. Recommendations should aim for a sweet spot between being on target and feeling invasive, while also offering room for unexpected content.

82. A word is worth a thousand pictures.

The problem with icons is that very few are so ubiquitous that they don't need a descriptive label. Which means that, in general, labels outperform icons.

- Icons can have different meanings in various interfaces. For example, a star might represent "favorites" in one context and "rating" in another, leading to confusion.
- When 100 percent clear, icons are not only visually appealing, but also are space-efficient and touch-friendly, transcending language barriers. They add to a cohesive visual narrative.
- But since most icons aren't 100 percent clear and not always consistent across interfaces, consider pairing them with labels or, at the very least, ensure consistent positioning for intuitive access.
- Users often rely on spatial memory when navigating: they might forget an icon's design but remember its position on the screen.
- In short, to ensure clarity and user-friendly navigation, it's best to combine the strength of both icons and descriptive labels.

83. Understand the sales funnel.

Discerning between B2C (business to consumer) and B2B (business to business) purchasing behaviors is vital because their objectives and processes diverge significantly.

- Individual buyers often make quick decisions, while companies take a methodical step-by-step approach.
- The B2B e-commerce journey is multilayered, from initial research to managerial assessments, ending with vendor selections.
- B2B pricing is seldom straightforward; when displayed, they're estimates influenced by factors like order volume and support.
- Even though B2B caters to businesses, the end users—everyday people—expect the same high-quality UX they encounter in B2C platforms. So, even in the B2B space, top-tier UX is nonnegotiable (see Principle 74).
- It's crucial to recognize the distinctions between B2C and B2B buying habits. B2B focuses on in-depth research, negotiations, and layered pricing, while B2C decisions are typically faster. However, top-tier user experience is vital for both.

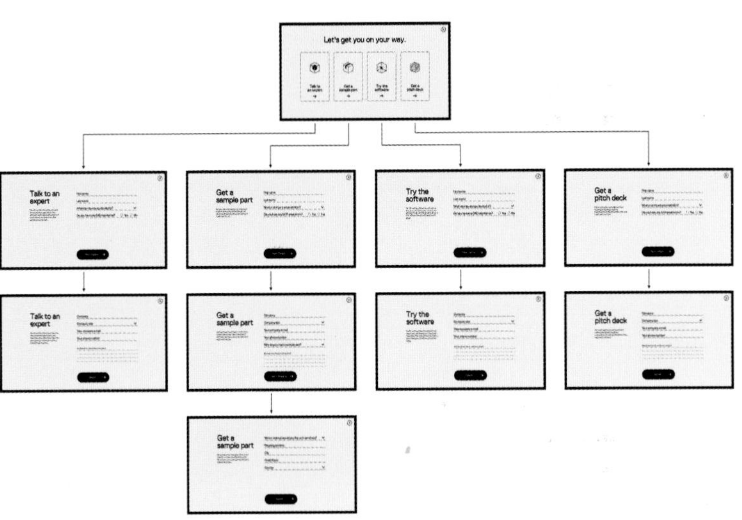

Markforged's industrial B2B 3D printer sales cycle is longer due to the significant manufacturing switch required of companies.

84. Target the right devices.

Recent data reveals that 50 percent of households worldwide have a desktop, but 75 percent of people own a smartphone. This indicates a shift in how people use and interact online, with smartphones accounting for about 60 percent of global internet use.

- Since 2009, the "mobile-first" design approach has taken center stage, emphasizing streamlining features instead of just miniaturizing desktop layouts.
- However, there's a risk: leaning too much into "mobile-first" can unintentionally lead to "mobile-only," causing designs to feel empty on larger screens or unfit for even tinier ones like smartwatches (see Principle 26).
- Let's remember: mobiles are for quick tasks on-the-go, while desktops are for deeper, focused work.
- The best way forward? Design with every device in mind. By understanding each device's pros and cons, we can craft experiences tailored for various screens and user scenarios.

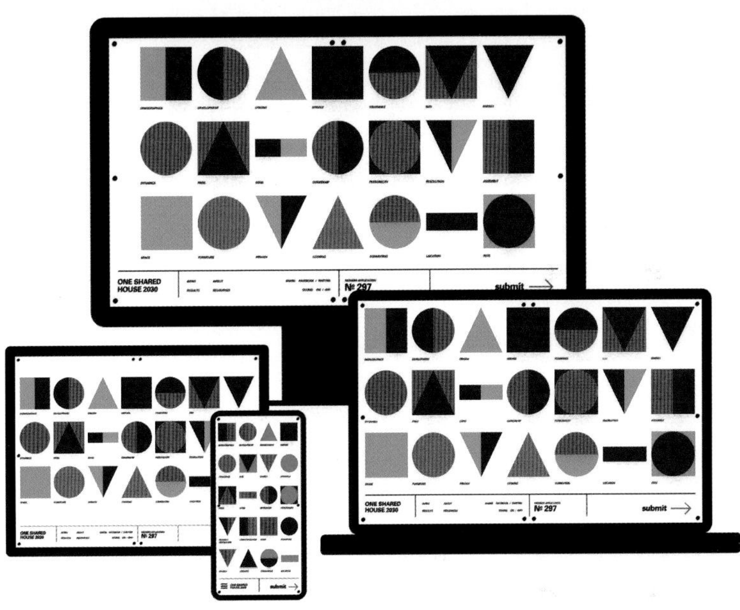

For "One Shared House 2030" with SPACE10 and IKEA, we designed for various devices considering screen sizes and usage contexts.

85. Systems are great for corporations.

In the early 2000s, small design studios relied on the now-defunct Flash technology for unique web designs. Before the advent of the iPhone and standardized design guidelines, there wasn't much consideration for varied screen sizes or accessibility, making updates challenging.

- Toward the end of the decade, mobile reigned supreme—which no longer supported Flash—and large corporations instead of small studios were now creating the majority of designs.
- And since bespoke design wasn't scalable, it paved the way for design systems.
- Design systems boost efficiency, make onboarding easier, and ensure users get a consistent experience every time.
- Tech giants like Microsoft and Google all standardized their digital design languages. But this approach can sometimes turn designers into mere assembly workers, taking away the creative freedom they once enjoyed.
- So there's a trade-off: design systems speed up processes and improve quality, but they curb the very creativity that fuels innovation in design.

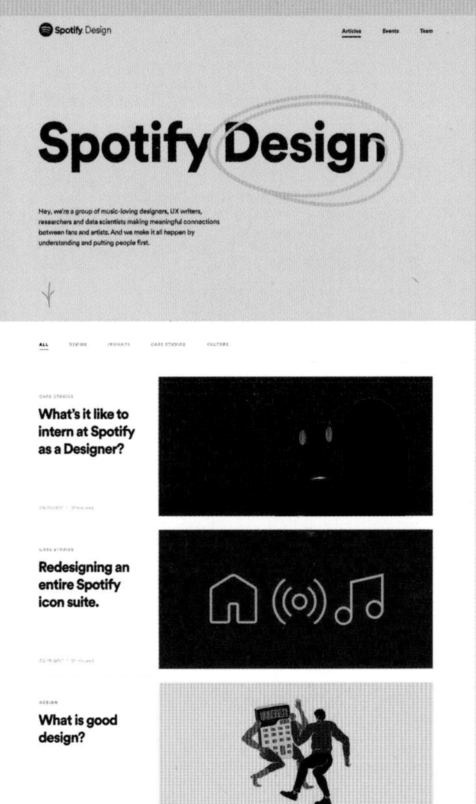

For corporations like Spotify, maintaining brand consistency across verticals outweighs a designer's personal expression.

86. Modularity is great for designers.

Many designers use a modular approach. After creating the main pages, they break them down into reusable components, forming a comprehensive system that encompasses the entire user experience.

- Modular design breaks things down into manageable pieces. This approach speeds up the creation of simple pages and lets designers focus on the more creative aspects.
- Using fewer unique templates saves time and establishes a consistent design rhythm that users easily recognize.
- These designs can be likened to LEGO blocks. Once these key components are set, they become the foundation for the entire user experience.
- It's vital to begin with a modular mindset. Although it requires some extra effort initially, it pays off in the long run.
- Simplifying complex tasks, accelerating page creation, and maintaining a consistent design rhythm for improved user recognition requires an initial investment, but offers greater creative freedom in design phases later on.

For M+ museum's site, we designed key screens, then broke them into reusable components for other pages.

87. Expect the unexpected.

Every design product is, in essence, a tool for the client. But simply having a tool isn't enough; it should be safeguarded against all possible scenarios that could affect the design in the future.

- The hallmark of a great design system is its ability to foresee extreme scenarios and embed contingency plans, ensuring a flawless user journey.
- A solid design system not only looks good but also anticipates the unexpected, having backup plans to guarantee a smooth user experience.
- Combining essential and additional modules with a clear design plan helps keep our designs consistent and true to our original concept, avoiding unexpected design changes.
- A strong design system anticipates future design challenges. By incorporating a clear "if this, then that" logic, it reduces the chances of clients unintentionally altering the design in ways it wasn't intended for.
- By marrying core and supplementary modules with a thoughtful design blueprint, it prevents unintended design deviations and ensures resilience in the face of future challenges.

An example of a normal news day on the *USA Today* website versus what the homepage would look like in the case of a national or international disaster

88. Voice assistants suck.

When we communicate with voice assistants, we engage with machine-learning algorithms that use natural language processing. But because communication is innate to us, we have high expectations for how that communication should work.

- Voice assistants aim to enhance our lives by simplifying tasks, improving accessibility, and even offering a touch of humanlike interaction. However, they often miss the mark, misunderstanding us more than we'd like.
- While they're great with straightforward instructions, they stumble when faced with the complexities of human language, like sarcasm or idioms.
- On top of that, at times, the exact wording needed for voice commands can be more time-consuming than just typing it manually.
- Seamless human–computer interaction is the dream, but it needs to be flawless every time. When communication with a voice assistant fails, not only does it remind us of the types of conversations we least enjoy, it makes us feel bad about ourselves.
- In short, achieving seamless human–computer interaction requires flawless performance every time to avoid negative user experiences, and we're not quite there yet.

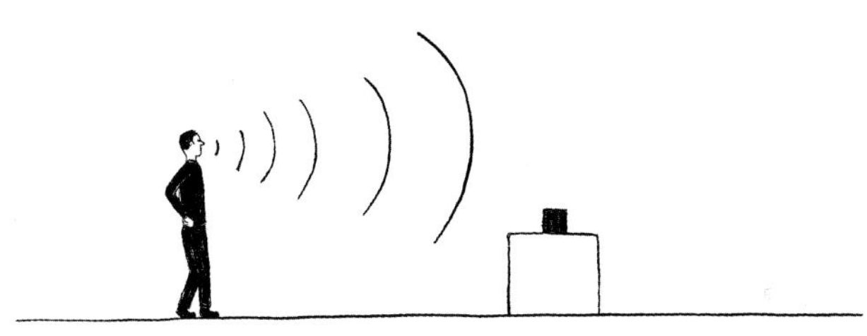

89. Don't ask for unnecessary things.

Users start tasks with a mental "decision battery," and bombarding them with too many choices can quickly drain it, potentially driving them away (see Principle 24).

- That's where the magic of defaults comes in. By preselecting options, we can lighten the decision-making load, letting users move forward with more ease and less room for error.
- We've got two main types of defaults. "Educated guesses" are like when a flight booking site knows your departure city. And "personalized defaults" tap into user data, such as filling in a regular payment amount.
- But, a heads-up: Avoid assuming sensitive information like gender and ethnicity, and steer clear of deceptive designs that might mislead.
- When done right, smart defaults not only improve the experience but also make users more likely to come back again.
- Using smart defaults, either from educated estimates or user data, can make decision-making easier for users and speed up their experience. But it's vital to handle sensitive information cautiously and be transparent to encourage trust.

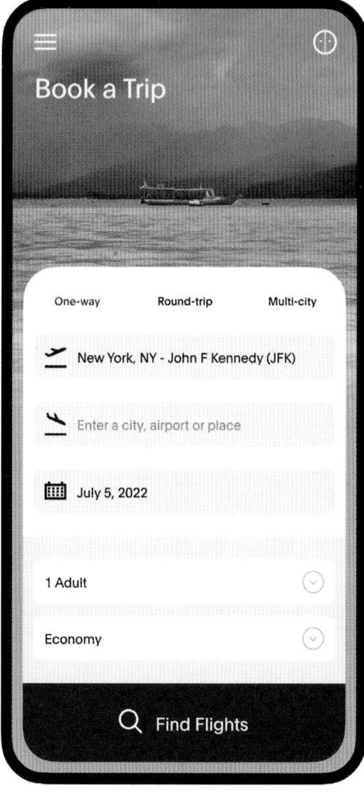

Prefilling form fields aid users, but it's important to avoid assumptions on sensitive information like gender.

90. Manage errors effectively.

Every UX designer has the responsibility to spot potential errors ahead of time so we can ensure people make as few errors as possible. Errors—or any kind of misunderstanding—are always the result of the system not being clear enough. They're never the fault of the user.

- Good design is all about anticipating and preventing user errors. That's why we have calendars blocking past dates, autocomplete features to catch typos, and dropdowns to guide choices.
- But errors can still happen, especially when users must type in information. When they stumble, it's essential users know how to fix things themselves.
- Effective error messages clearly highlight the problem, explain why it happened, and offer a solution—all in the place where the hiccup occurred.
- When system glitches are out of the user's hands, being transparent about what's happening and providing an estimated fix time can make all the difference.
- Clear communication minimizes frustration and helps users avoid that dreaded call to customer service.

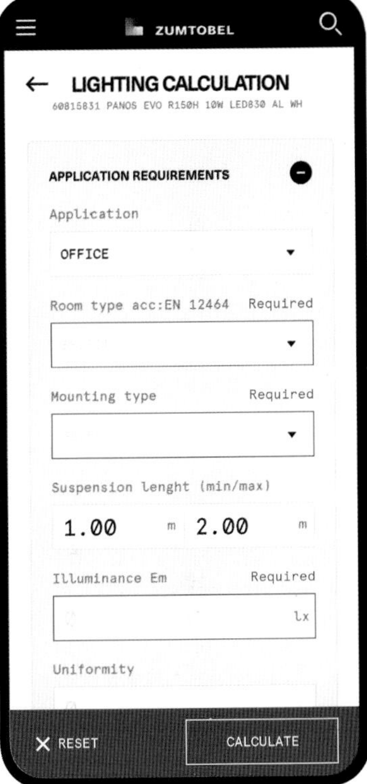

Ensure systems provide clear feedback on errors, indicating if users can resolve them or if they're system-related.

91. Accept many inputs.

When designing interfaces, embracing a flexible approach to user inputs is vital. The ethos of accepting varied inputs, be it case sensitivity or file types, has been the cornerstone of the internet as we know it today.

- The spirit of the early internet was all about inclusivity: different computer systems, regardless of their protocols, should be able to chat with one another.
- We owe a lot to Jon Postel, an American computer scientist. When working on the TCP protocol, he believed in smooth operations over perfection with his "Be conservative in what you do, be liberal in what you accept from others" mantra.
- This philosophy also shaped how we handle HTML, instead of showing nothing, the aim was to display even the not-so-perfect HTML.
- This mindset also found its way into UX design, especially when users fill out forms, where we are broadly accepting of various input types.
- This adaptable way of handling user inputs, inspired by the early internet's inclusive spirit, is one of the things that has led to a more user-friendly and inclusive online experience for all.

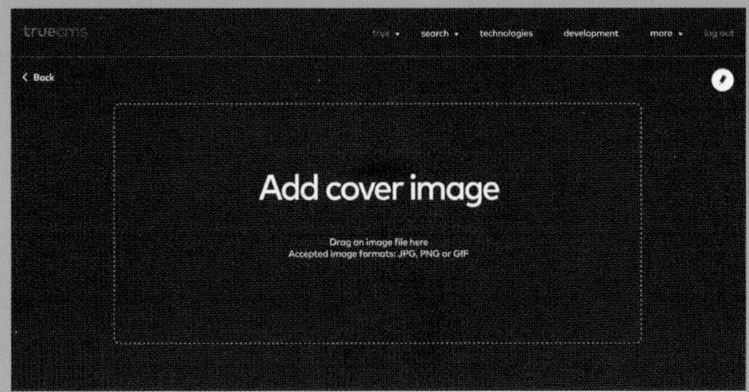

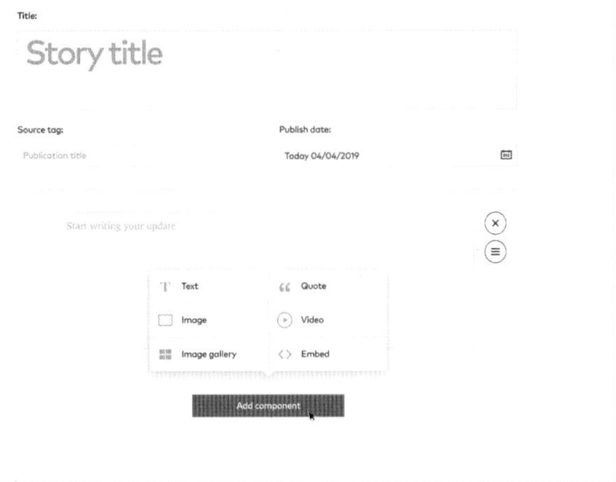

In the CMS for True, we enabled various image type uploads for new pages to reduce potential errors.

92. Confirm user actions.

Effective user interfaces prioritize clear confirmation prompts. Without them, users often navigate in uncertainty, leading to additional steps or even unintended consequences.

- Confirmations play a double role: they reassure users about their actions and, in some cases, act as a safety net against accidental choices (see Principle 14).
- But it's all about balance. Major decisions definitely need that double-check. But for small, easy-to-fix stuff, maybe just an "undo" button is sufficient. We don't want to bombard people with endless "Are you sure?" pop-ups.
- Being crystal clear with labeling and instructions is very important. In particular, when it comes to action buttons think "Confirm delete" versus simply "Confirm."
- If we are in any way ambiguous about our instructions, users can get flustered, they might end up doing something they didn't intend to do, and trust in our product takes a hit.
- Clear confirmation prompts in user interfaces serve the dual purpose of reassuring users and preventing accidental actions, but striking a balance between necessary confirmations for major decisions and simplified interactions for minor tasks is crucial.

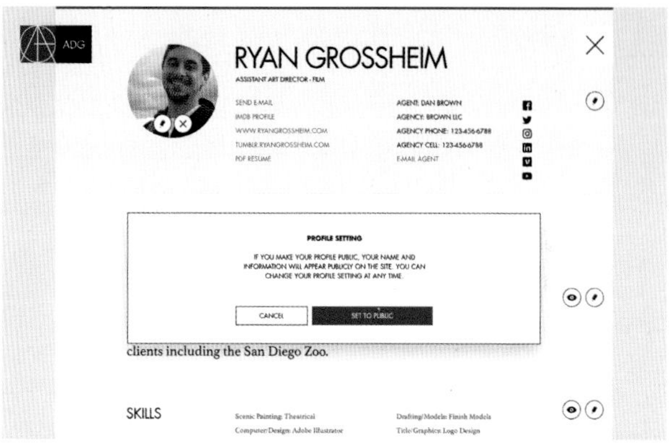

Examples of confirmation pop-ups that let the user know when the consequences of their actions are severe or irreversible.

93. Broken pages shouldn't feel broken.

Error pages, especially the infamous 404, are an integral aspect of a user's online experience. When a user encounters a broken link or a missing page, the 404 error is what they'll often see.

- A 404-error page shouldn't be an afterthought. It's an opportunity to exhibit the brand's personality and can even allow companies to showcase their sense of humor.
- Stumbling onto a creative 404 is like finding a hidden gem in a video game—it's a delightful surprise and adds a splash of fun to the user's day.
- The best 404s are those playful nudges that make users smile, making a slip-up feel more like a secret handshake with the brand.
- But let's not forget functionality. While a touch of humor is great, these pages should also steer users back on track, helping them find what they were after or suggesting an alternative—always better than leaving them at a dead end.
- In short, error pages, such as the 404 error, are an opportunity to add a touch of fun. However, while creativity is essential, these pages should also serve their primary function of guiding users back on track or offering alternatives to avoid leaving them at a dead end.

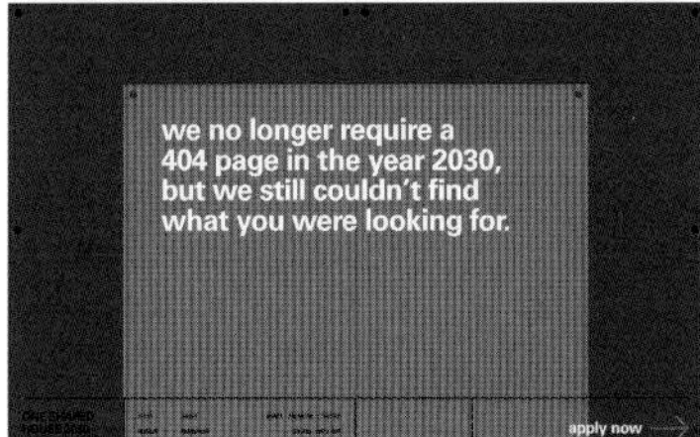

Your 404 pages should prioritize accessibility, and main navigation and search functions should prevent user dead ends.

94. Fill the gap imagination can't bridge.

It's easy to imagine what it might feel like when we press a button to go to another page or how an image carousel might transition, but it's harder to imagine more complicated interactions that rely on new or unusual interaction patterns.

- Crafting an authentic user experience dives deeper than just visuals; it's about the emotional and tactile journey users embark on with the interface of the product.
- Sketches and wireframes are great for mapping out the basics, but they fall short in capturing the actual "feel" of interactions.
- To truly grasp the sensation of, say, a button's responsiveness, interactive prototypes are game-changers, letting users dive into the full experience.
- In essence, when traditional design tools fall short in capturing the authentic user experience and the "feel" of interactions, interactive prototypes become essential for users to fully grasp and engage with the design's vibe, going beyond just visuals and exploring the emotional and tactile journey users embark on with the product's interface.

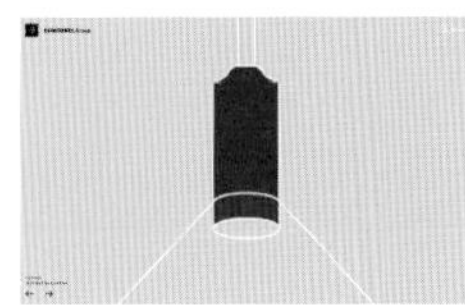

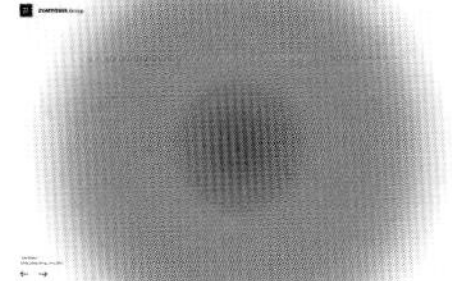

We prototyped interactive homepage covers for Zumtobel, ensuring interactions were appropriate and not annoying.

95. Metric-based design is silly.

The notorious incident where Google chose to test forty-one shades of blue, ultimately resulting in the departure of its leading designer, Doug Bowman, to Twitter, highlights the struggle of metrics versus intuition in design.

- Design is a dance between hard numbers and creative intuition. Metrics give us measurable results but over-relying on them risks losing design's unique heart and soul (see Principle 52).
- Just because a design tweak boosts user engagement doesn't mean it's the only factor at play; many variables can shape those numbers.
- Think about color. It's perceived differently depending on the device settings and individual perceptions, making strict data-driven decisions tricky.
- The real magic happens when we blend data insights with the seasoned intuition and expertise of design pros.
- In essence, design is a delicate balance between hard metrics and creative intuition. Relying solely on metrics can risk losing the unique essence of design, as many variables influence measurable results. The true magic occurs when data insights harmonize with the seasoned intuition and expertise of design professionals.

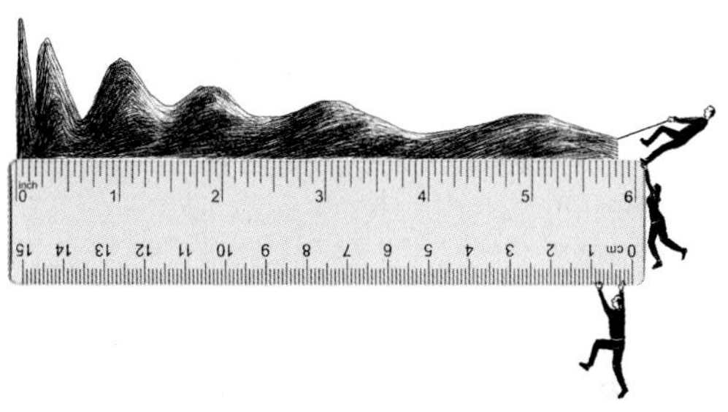
inch
0 1 2 3 4 5 6
0 cm 1 2 3 4 5 6 7 8 9 10 11 12 13 14 15

96. Most issues can be spotted a mile ahead.

Usability tests aim to evaluate the efficiency and user-friendliness of a design by analyzing both qualitative and quantitative aspects of user interactions. This process acts as a safety net, aiming to ensure a flawless user experience before a product's public debut.

- Usability testing involves observing participants as they complete set tasks, providing designers with insights into user perceptions and facilitating adjustments based on immediate feedback.
- Experienced professionals often find usability test outcomes predictable, suggesting the primary value lies in validation rather than new discoveries.
- Notable shifts in usability test outcomes arise when designers explore unfamiliar areas, such as new devices, platforms, or unique target demographics.
- While usability tests were crucial during the digital era's early stages, their significance for familiar designs and audiences diminishes as expertise and standardization advance.
- Ultimately, usability testing's primary value lies in validation and ensuring a flawless user experience.

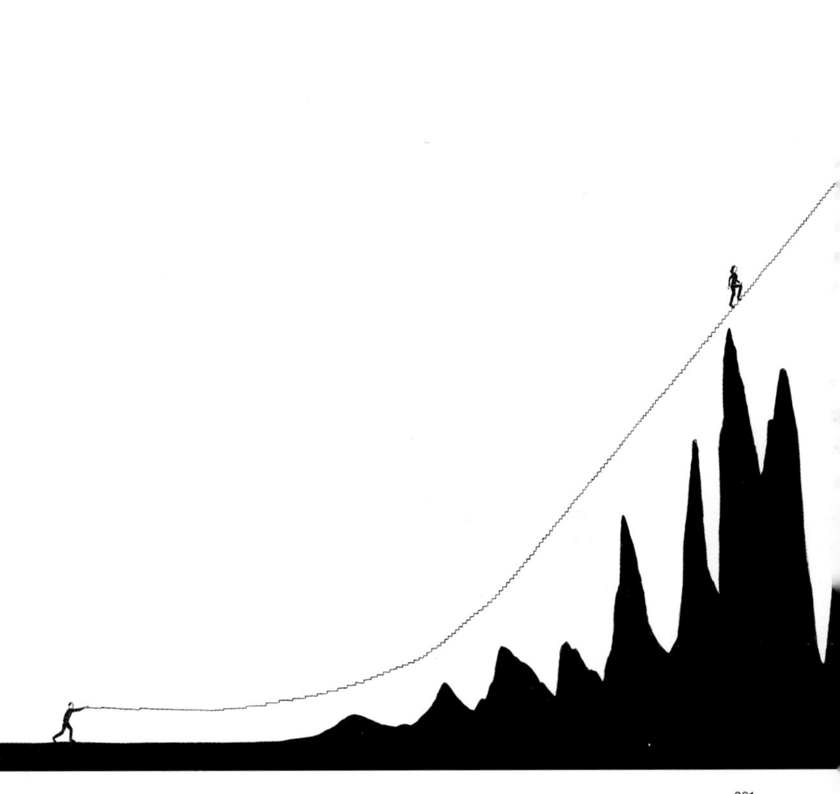

97. Don't grade your own homework.

The challenge of evaluating one's own designs with objectivity is universal, transcending levels of experience and expertise in the design world. It underscores the profound influence of inherent biases on our perceptions and judgments.

- Designers testing their own work often lean toward validation, potentially missing alternative views due to inherent biases.
- Both novice and seasoned designers can fall prey to this, reflecting our natural inclination to seek affirmation and sidestep critique.
- The emotional investment in a project can hinder objective evaluations, as designers deeply connect with their work.
- To ensure genuine feedback, it's beneficial to separate the roles of creator and evaluator, providing a fresh perspective and promoting user-centric results.
- In essence, the challenge of evaluating one's own designs objectively is universal and influenced by inherent biases.

98. Get the most bang for your buck.

Prioritizing areas of a product based on user engagement is essential in optimizing the user experience. Focusing on the most frequently used sections can have a transformative impact on overall user satisfaction.

- The Pareto principle suggests that around 80 percent of results come from roughly 20 percent of causes; in UX, this means most user activities are centered on a particular feature subset.
- Therefore, it's important to focus on the platform or product areas with the most user activity, as interactions are typically concentrated in specific features or sections.

- Rely on user behavior analytics for evidence-based decisions rather than just initial instincts.
- By targeting these high-engagement areas, enhancements will benefit most users, optimizing both return on investment and timely updates.
- In short, prioritizing product areas based on user engagement, following the Pareto principle, can significantly impact overall user satisfaction. Focusing on high-engagement sections, guided by user behavior analytics, leads to evidence-based decisions that benefit the majority of users, optimizing ROI and timely updates.

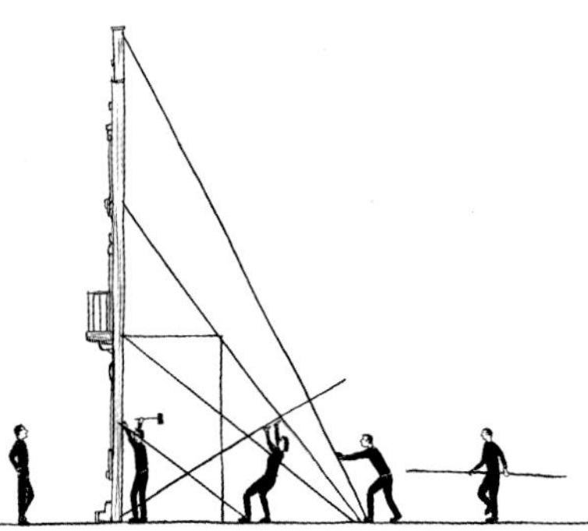

99. Stay involved post-launch.

There are no laws that say client projects have to end with launch. If the people who worked on the product keep an eye on how it's doing months or even years after it has gone live, potential problems can be spotted before they even occur.

- True commitment to a project extends beyond just launching it; the real work involves maintaining its design for years after.
- A project truly thrives when nurtured post-launch, ensuring it stays relevant and adaptable in today's fast-paced market.
- Studios that go beyond a "launch-and-leave" approach, offering regular, even if intermittent, oversight can significantly elevate a product's success.
- Continual involvement with an emphasis on user needs ensures that the product remains user-centric, regardless of changing company goals or market trends (see Principle 17).
- After launching, continued involvement is key to sustained success. It's essential to update and adjust the design to keep the product user-focused and current in an ever-evolving market. Studios that keep an eye out post-launch help ensure the product continues to thrive over time.

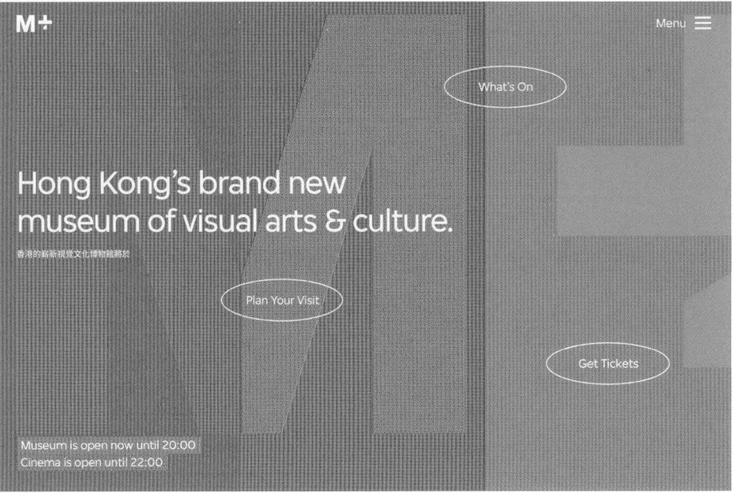

Since launching M+ museum's site in 2021, we continuously collaborate, ensuring user goals, new initiatives, and a healthy codebase.

100. Lower expectations for high satisfaction.

Navigating through a project's life cycle can feel a bit like an intricate acrobatic sequence where every move matters. If one person messes up, it has disastrous consequences for everyone else.

- Starting a project means anticipating potential challenges, which includes evaluating risks and preparing for unforeseen hurdles.
- Staying in sync is key. Despite careful planning, unforeseen issues can arise, but quick responses keep things on course.
- Reflecting after completion provides invaluable insights, helping teams prepare more effectively for future challenges.
- It's best to be prepared for all outcomes. While we hope for smooth project progress, it's important to be ready for surprises. So, instead of assuming everything will go perfectly, let's be realistic and protect ourselves from potential setbacks.
- During a project, it's crucial to expect challenges, assess potential risks, and be ready for surprises. Learning from past projects helps in future planning. By being realistic from the start and preparing for all outcomes, we can better manage projects and handle unforeseen issues.

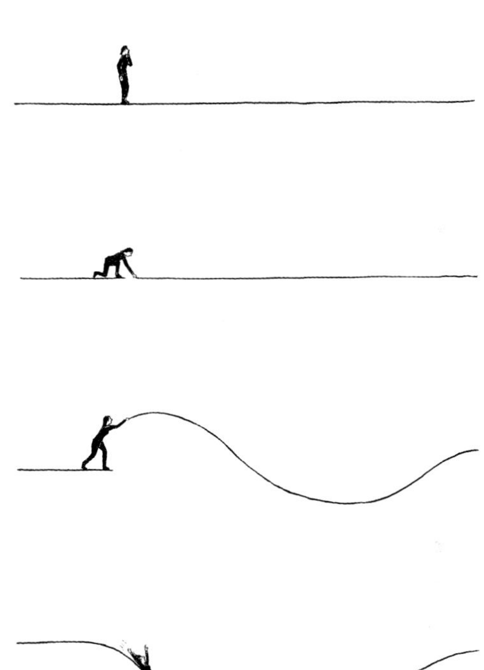

About the Author

Irene Pereyra, co-founder of Brooklyn's "Anton & Irene" studio, has led UX strategies for renowned clients like the Met Museum, *USA Today*, Spotify, Google, and SPACE10/IKEA since 2007. The studio also spends three months a year on self-initiated design projects under which the interactive documentary "One Shared House", and the NU:RO analog watch. Her awarded works have been showcased globally, and she's spoken at over 100 international design conferences. Irene lectures at institutions like SVA and Hyper Island, and is the chair of Interaction Design at Harbour.Space in Barcelona and Bangkok. She has an M.S. in Communications Design from Pratt Institute.

Acknowledgments

This book—along with all the stories in this book—wouldn't have been possible without the constant support of my design partner, and studio co-founder, Anton Repponen. Two more people are responsible for making this book eminently more readable and understandable—my editor Jonathan Simcosky and the illustrator Vincent Broquaire. But most importantly, this book is dedicated to my students, who for years have helped me clarify and sharpen my understanding of the complex, expansive, and evolving field we have chosen to dedicate ourselves to. If their curiosity, enthusiasm, and empathy are an indication of the future of user experience design, it's a bright future indeed.

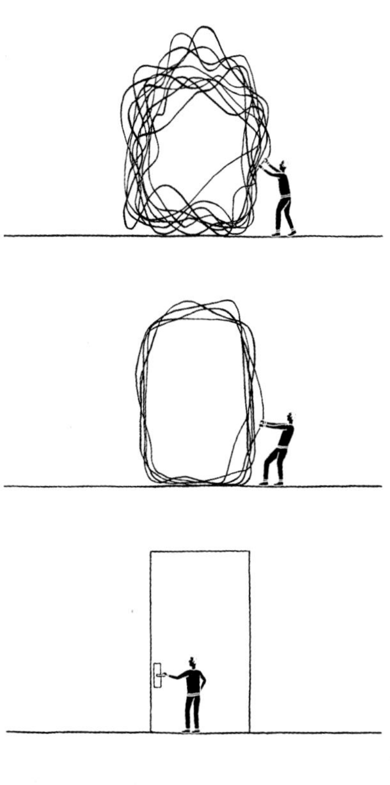

Quarto.com

First published in 2024 by Rockport Publishers, an imprint of The Quarto Group, 100 Cummings Center, Suite 265-D, Beverly, MA 01915, USA.
T (978) 282-9590 F (978) 283-2742

Rockport Publishers titles are also available at discount for retail, wholesale, promotional, and bulk purchase. For details, contact the Special Sales Manager by email at specialsales@quarto.com or by mail at The Quarto Group, Attn: Special Sales Manager, 100 Cummings Center, Suite 265-D, Beverly, MA 01915, USA.

10 9 8 7 6 5 4 3 2 1

ISBN: 978-0-7603-8803-7

Digital edition published in 2024
eISBN: 978-0-7603-8804-4

Library of Congress Cataloging-in-Publication Data available

Design: Anton Repponen and Irene Pereyra
Cover Image: Vincent Broquaire
Page Layout: Anton Repponen and Irene Pereyra
Illustration: Vincent Broquaire

Printed in China